Give God the Glory!

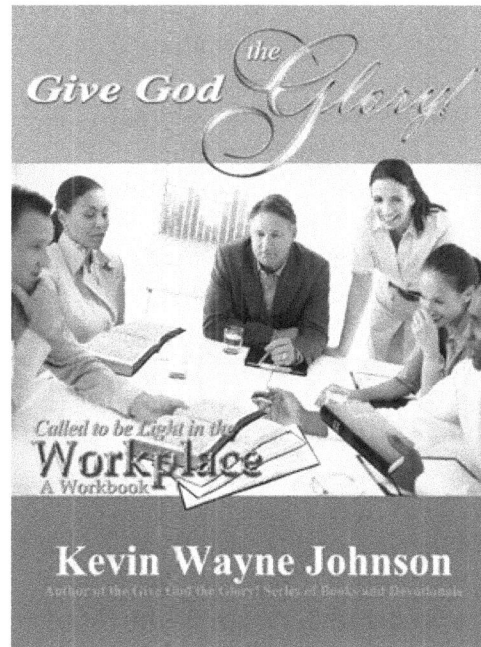

Give God *the Glory!*

Called to be *Light* in the
Workplace
A Workbook

Kevin Wayne Johnson

Author of the Give God the Glory! Series of Books and Devotionals

Called to be *Light* in the Workplace

A Workbook

Give God the Glory! Series

Other books by Kevin Wayne Johnson

As Principal Author:

Give God the Glory! Called to be Light in the Workplace, 2003
Second printing

Give God the Glory! Let Your Light So Shine (a devotional), 2004 & 2012 (Revised/Republished)
Fourth printing
[Also available in print-on-demand, Amazon.com Kindle, and e-book formats]

Give God the Glory! The Godly Family Life, 2005
Second printing
[Also available in print-on-demand, Amazon.com Kindle, and e-book formats]

Give God the Glory! Your Role in Your Family (a devotional), 2006
Second printing
[Also available in print-on-demand, Amazon.com Kindle, and e-book formats]

Give God the Glory! Know God and Do the Will of God Concerning Your Life
STUDY GUIDE, 2008
[Also available in print-on-demand, Amazon.com Kindle, and e-book formats]

Give God the Glory! The Power in the Local Church, 2010
[Also available in print-on-demand, Amazon.com Kindle, and e-book formats]

Give God the Glory! Know God & Do the Will of God Concerning Your Life
(Revised Edition), 2011
[Also available in print-on-demand, Amazon.com Kindle, and e-book formats]

As Contributing Author:

No Limits ... No Boundaries: Marketing Your Book Globally to Maximize Sales, 2009
[e-book]

Blended Families, An Anthology, 2006
[Christian Small Publishers Association 2008 Non-Fiction Book of the Year]

The Secret: How His Word Impacts Our Lives, 2007

Give God the Glory!

Called to be *Light*
in the Workplace

A Workbook

Kevin Wayne Johnson

Writing for the Lord
M I N I S T R I E S

www.writingforthelord.org / www.writingforthelord.com

Give God the Glory! series
Called to be Light in the Workplace—A Workbook
Retail Price: $15.00
Copyright © 2013 by Kevin Wayne Johnson
First Printing

Cover Concept by Kevin Wayne Johnson
Cover Design by The Mazzocchi Group © 2013
Zendra Manley, Chief Executive Officer and Graphic Designer
Three Rivers, MI
1 (877) 842-6916

Edited and Designed by Hallagen Ink
Tanya Brockett, MBA, Crozet, VA
1 (434) 409-7058
www.HallagenInk.com

Distributed throughout the United States, Canada, and internationally by:
  (1) Send the Light Distribution
       100 Biblica Way
       Elizabethton, TN 37643 USA
       1 (800) 289-2772
       1 (800) 759-2779 (fax)
       1 (888) 785-2432 Stock Check
       www.stl-distribution.com
  (2) Amazon.com, Barnes & Noble Booksellers, and eleven other strategic global distribution
       partners in the USA, United Kingdom, France, Spain, South America, and Australia.

Unless otherwise noted, all scripture references are taken from the King James Version (KJV) of *The Holy Bible*, The New Open Bible Study Edition, Thomas Nelson, Incorporated, 1990. Other versions throughout this Workbook include the New International Version (NIV), Amplified Version (AMP), New Living Translation (NLT), New Century Version (NCV), the New King James Version (NKJV), The Message (MSG), and New International Reader's Version (NIRV), taken from BibleGateway.com.

ISBN: 978- 0-9705902-7-5

Library of Congress Catalog Number: 2013941845

Printed in the United States of America

Celebrating
Twelve Years of
Publishing
Excellence

Writing for the Lord Ministries

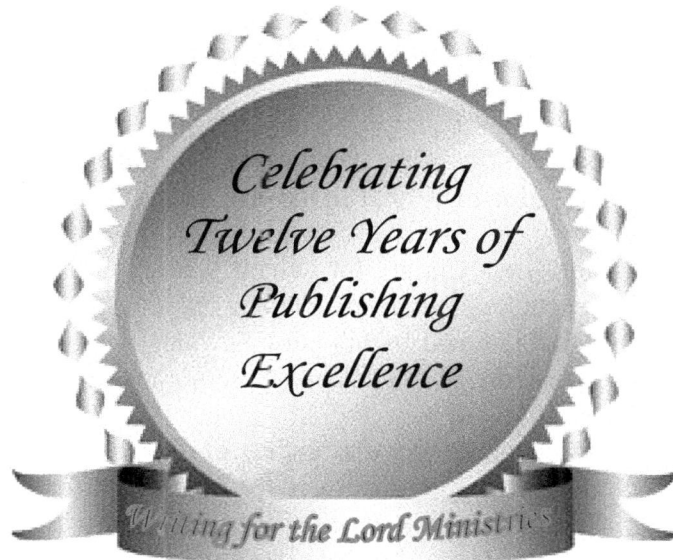

This *Workbook* is based upon the original contents contained in Book #2 in the series:
Give God the Glory! Called to be Light in the Workplace
Here is what some reviewers from around the country have to say about *Give God the Glory!*

"*Give God the Glory!* Called to be *Light* in the Workplace is a nice blend of spiritual and practical wisdom about being the best ambassador for Christ in the workplace. I especially like the servant leader section and the material about being an effective communicator. Readers will be stirred to press on toward the mark to win the prize (i.e., Christ) for which we are called heavenward. Mr. Johnson challenges our complacency and encourages us to maintain a "new wineskin heart" into which our Lord can pour much of the "new wine" that is found in this book."

—**Jim Biscardi, Jr.**, *President, New Jersey Christian Ministries, Incorporated*

"In my professional role as editor, book coach, and author of five of my own books, I am immensely impressed with Brother Kevin Johnson's latest work, *Give God the Glory!* Called to be *Light* in the Workplace. Not only is the content of the book especially helpful to me as a leader who has mentored many women over the past twenty-five years, but the structure of the book is outstanding. The quotes, graphics, and illustrations are excellent. Above all, I appreciate that which he has presented as possible solutions to our day-to-day challenges in the workplace. Taking one of his personal quotes from the book, let me say this: 'Excellence never happens by accident. We have to make it happen.' Kevin has made it happen with his latest educational tool. It needs to be on every employer's shelf."

—**Minister M.D. Edwards**, *Founder and President,*
The Called and Ready Writers, Detroit, Michigan

"Simplistically clear and incisive, a real need for the 21st century working world."

—**Melvin Johnson, Sr.** *(deceased), Founder and Pastor,*
True Disciple Ministries, Somerville, New Jersey

"Many authors have written about surviving and thriving in the workplace. There have also been many books written on being a Christian light. However, few if any books have effectively integrated these two important topics into an inspiring and very useful book. Mr. Johnson is successful in this endeavor. His new work is very meaningful in a challenging and chaotic work environment. He challenges employees to be Christian lights on their respective jobs. Through a comprehensive analysis of the Bible and the three phases of career progression, Mr. Johnson reminds employees that God is in the workplace."

—**Diane Floyd Sutton**, *President, Sutton Enterprises and Author of*
Increasing the Spirit and Effectiveness of People in the Workplace, *Washington, DC*

"Kevin's knowledge of the Lord and writing are incomparable to anyone I've met in the industry plus his spirit is so warm and open—he is a true servant of the Lord. Very inspiring!"

—**Pam Perry**, *President, American Christian Writers, Detroit chapter*

"The principle purpose—God made man for His glory! As you think of that concept, how much do we really understand what the glory of God is all about? How does the glory of God relate to our everyday life? Kevin Johnson has presented to us how we can glorify God not only in church but also in the workplace. It is of vital importance that we grasp this principle that has been presented for us in Kevin's intriguing work called, "Give God the Glory!" May this be the pursuit of all of us as we think of the very purpose God had for us as He placed us on planet Earth."

—**Joe Jordan**, *Executive Director, Word of Life Fellowship, Inc.,*
Schroon Lake, New York

"You're in a store thinking about buying this book. You ask yourself two logical questions: 'Is it worth spending $15 to read what this man has to say about being a Christian in the workplace? Will I feel that I received my money's worth when I finish this book?' The answer is a resounding YES! Kevin Johnson has taken the Word of God, blended it with years of experience in government and corporations, seasoned it with helpful quotations, examples and resources, and baked it in the fire of the Holy Spirit to cook up a very relevant book. I believe that, in God's economy, the $15 you choose to invest in *Give God the Glory: Called to be Light in the Workplace* can deliver a profoundly positive and eternal return-on-investment."

—**Drew Crandall**, *President, Northeast Christians at Work,*
Vernon, Connecticut

Award-Winning *Give God the Glory!* Series

Winner of eighteen literary/media awards since 2001 with selected books available in the Urdu, Falam, Ngawn, Swahili, Hungarian, Georgian, Creole, and French languages

NAACP WWW.NAACP.ORG	43rd Annual NAACP Image Award Nominee (Literature): Best Instructional Book 2012
Aspicomm MEDIA	Best Spiritual / Inspirational Book and Trailblazer Award 2010
International Book Awards **FINALIST** InternationalBookAwards.com	International Best Books Award Finalist—Religion: Christianity USA Book News & JPX Media 2010
Best Books Award FINALIST! USA Book News	National Best Books Award Finalist—Religion: Christianity USA Book News & JPX Media 2009
Books & Authors .net - Award for - *Literary Excellence*	Award for Literary Excellence 2008

Our books have been reviewed and endorsed by The Dove Foundation.

Dove.org FAMILY APPROVED **ALL AGES**

If any man speak, let him speak as the oracles of God; if any man minister, let him do it as of the ability which God giveth: **that God in all things may be glorified** *through Jesus Christ, to whom be praise and dominion for ever and ever. A-men.*

—1 Peter 4:11 KJV

Whoever speaks, [let him do it as one who utters] oracles of God; whoever renders service, [let him do it] as with the strength which God furnishes abundantly, so **that in all things God may be glorified** *through Jesus Christ (the Messiah). To Him be the glory and dominion forever and ever (through endless ages). Amen (so be it).*

—1 Peter 4:11 Amplified

Foundational Scripture (emphasis added)—*Writing for the Lord* Ministries, LLC

Writing for the Lord
M I N I S T R I E S

This *Workbook* is dedicated to the loving memory of my mother, Adele. Mom departed this life on Sunday afternoon, March 18, 2001, at approximately 3:00 PM. I thank you, Mom, for your *light* that shined brightly during the sixty-two years that God placed you on this earth. You left a deposit in my life and have encouraged me to let my *light* so shine before men, that they may see the goodness of God. Thank you for the memories. *I love you.*

Glory!

A divine quality. Literally meaning heavy or weighty.

It represents the brightness, splendor, and radiance of God's presence as well as His visible revelation of Himself.

Our word 'doxology' comes from 'doxa,' the Greek word for Glory.

Contents

*Ye are the **light** of the world. A city that is set on an hill cannot be hid. Neither do men light a candle, and put it under a bushel, but on a candlestick; and it giveth **light** unto all that are in the house.*

—Matthew 5:14–15 KJV

You are the light that gives light to the world. A city that is built on a hill cannot be hidden. And people don't hide a light under a bowl. They put it on a lampstand so the light shines for all the people in the house.

—Matthew 5:14–15 New Century Version (NCV)

Preface

I love God because He first loved me. I am eternally grateful for the marvelous things that He has done for my wife and I on our respective jobs over the past twenty-five to thirty years. ***Give God the Glory!*** *Called to be Light in the Workplace—A Workbook* is the eighth book in this series about God's goodness to His children in different stages of our lives. Through these pages, I intend to demonstrate, by the Word of God, that within the three stages of our work life—the beginning (intern or trainee), journeyman (mid-level manager), and mentor (leader and senior executive)—that God calls us to be *light* in the workplace at every step along the way. I will educate each reader to recognize the dangers that Satan puts in the way of God's children and how our response to these dangers separates us from those who choose to walk in darkness. Our *light* must shine and always illuminate on our jobs to give others hope as well as the desire, and courage, to uphold ethical, Godly, and disciplined behavior during the forty to sixty hours that we traditionally work each week. To this end, we are commissioned and called by God, through Jesus Christ, to be distinctively different and to excel at what we do. Our jobs are a resource, but God is our source. As long as we stay connected to Him, we have assurance through His Word concerning the guarantee of peace and tranquility to achieve our dreams: *"but with God all things are possible"* (Matthew 19:26). When God calls us to do something, He also equips us to handle the job and the challenges that we will face (Romans 11:29).

It has been said many times over and over and over again, but bears repeating—We have more in common than we have differences. We all rely upon our intellect, body strength, athleticism, charisma, and work ethic to earn a living. Simply put, we must work for the money that we earn in order to sustain ourselves during our lifetime. In the first chapter of Genesis, verse 26, God's first commandment to Adam was to *dress* and *keep* the Garden of Eden. Translation: Work! The creator designed His creation to work and that is the primary means by which we earn money to pay for the necessities of life: shelter, clothes, food, transportation, health care, and education. Work is a necessity of life, and God's Word says *"if you don't work, you don't eat"* (2 Thessalonians 3:10).

Our jobs bring interesting and sometimes extremely frustrating challenges into our lives. How we choose to respond to the never-ending challenges at work is the key to what separates those who enjoy promotions and those who do not. Needless to say, the workplace is a very competitive environment. Most of our colleagues, bosses, subordinates, and peers are continually seeking more money, more attractive benefits, and better overall opportunities at work, often within the organization or company where they are currently working. You stand in their way. This competitive spirit, manifested outwardly, is satanic and promotes self-centered and selfish behavior as seen through people at different stages in their life or career. Satan is an accuser of our brethren (Revelation 12:10), is wicked (Matthew 13:9), is a deceiver (Revelation 20:10), is our adversary (1 Peter 5:8), and is the ruler of this world (Ephesians 6:12). He is real! Subconsciously unaware of their conduct, most people tend to think more of themselves than they do about others without realizing what the effect of their behavior has on people within their sphere of influence.

I officially entered the workforce in the summer of 1984 following a year of disappointing unemployment. Since that time, I have survived a myriad of changes that have taken place within the federal government as well as corporate America. The majority of these changes have been unannounced, frequent, continual, self-serving, unproductive, detrimental to the workforce, and devastating to individuals and families alike. Countless numbers of people have not been able to cope while others are left bitter and have chosen to underachieve. Thus, many have failed to fulfill their God-ordained purpose during their lifetime.

In the Book of Matthew, chapter five, six, and seven, Jesus' first public sermon during His public ministry focuses on teaching us how to live within the kingdom of God. Jesus clearly demonstrates that there is a distinction between *how to earn a living* (how we make money to survive) and *how to live* (persistent application of Godly principles to everyday life). In these passages of scripture, Jesus teaches His disciples, and a multitude that have gathered at a mountain on the edge of the Sea of Galilee, about attitude, and how to be *light* and salt. History reveals that this mountain is probably one of the hills northwest of Capernaum, for shortly after this Sermon on the Mount, we find Jesus and His disciples entering that city. These character traits are explained in detail by a masterful teacher who used parables as the object lesson(s) for the purpose of extracting a spiritual meaning from the natural examples He used. I have always found it interesting and insightful that Jesus would focus on these three key character traits at the outset of His first message during His three and one-half years of public ministry. This was His trial discourse. What follows are God-centered and ethical principles on to how to live a successful life on earth during our entire lifetime, including in the workplace.

Now, let's **Give God the Glory!** …

Kevin Wayne Johnson

Acknowledgements

I give thanks to God Almighty, first and foremost, for the wonderful blessings that shower me each and every day. I openly and unashamedly acknowledge my personal relationship with Him, through Jesus Christ, as the reason for my joy, peace, prosperity, and good health.

Thank you Gail as we celebrated our twentieth wedding anniversary on March 6, during the same month of the original release of my second book in this series (*Called to be Light in the Workplace*). Your support has encouraged me to continue to write. Together, let's **Give God the Glory!** continually and for the remainder of our time together on earth as husband and wife. Thanks to my three sons, Kevin, Christopher, and Cameron, for being such great sons and making me a proud father. I love you all more each day.

Thank you Dad for your strength since mom's death and your voice of support. It is always comforting to hear words of encouragement from one's Dad. I appreciate all of the book sales and word of mouth endorsements that you generated throughout the Richmond, Virginia community.

To Steve Gilliland for inspiring me and challenging me back in 2000 in New York City to write from the heart. Steve was the spark that lit my initial fire to write!! Tanya Brockett at Hallagen Ink for the outstanding editing and formatting services over the years. Kings Highway Web Design for the incredible website development and management to promote my global presence. To our Winning Writers ministry at CELEBRATION CHURCH @ Columbia (Maryland). The fun and fellowship is awesome! To my website and Facebook marketing team at Web.com. You are all very special and uniquely positioned to positively impact the lives of millions.

To all of the book editors, reviewers, bookstore owners and managers, publishing organizations and associations, public relations professionals, radio and television personalities, churches, clergy, family and friends, thank you for what you have taught me over the past twelve years as I continually grow and mature in this global publishing industry. Your love, devotion, prayers, encouragement, support, counsel, mentoring, and advice, have made me a better writer and laborer for the Lord. Thank you!

*Then spake Jesus again unto them, saying, I am the **light** of the world: he that followeth me shall not walk in darkness, but shall have the **light** of life.*

—John 8:12 KJV

*When Jesus spoke again to the people, he said, I am the **light** of the world. Whoever follows me will never walk in darkness, but will have the **light** of life.*

—John 8:12 NIV

Introduction

*D*uring my thirty years in the workplace, twenty-seven with the federal government and three and one-half within the setting of corporate America, I have seen friends, peers, associates, and colleagues at all levels within the organization encounter multiple problems while at work. I, too, have faced them. In most instances, the affected persons feel isolated, alone, and trapped with nowhere to turn. You are NOT alone.

Give God the Glory! *Called to be Light in the Workplace—A Workbook* exposes the challenges that *many* people face on the job. Throughout the history of this country, there has been tremendous change in the workplace. America has shifted from an agricultural society (late 1600s to 1880), to an industrial society (1890 to 1980), to an information society (1985 to present). Keeping pace with these constant changes is a full-time job in and of itself. Having a personal relationship with God, through Jesus Christ, is the assurance that we can overcome all of the pressure and change that is inherent to a typical day at work.

The subtitle is the heart of this Workbook, yet the desired objective is to fully recognize and acknowledge our responsibility to ***Give God the Glory!*** *Called* is defined as "my desire to do." In the original Greek language, *kaleō*, which is derived from the root *kal-*, means "to call anyone, invite, summon," particularly of the divine call to partake of the blessing of redemption and of nomenclature or vocation. *Light*, *phōs*, derives from roots *pha-* and *phan-* in the original Greek language. In this context, man, naturally, is incapable of receiving spiritual light inasmuch as he lacks the capacity for spiritual things. Hence, believers are called "sons of light" not merely because they have received a revelation from God, but because in the New Birth they have received the spiritual capacity for it. The word "light" is referenced in *The Holy Bible* 264 times! Light is characterized as an element that:

Illuminates	Shines
Exposes Darkness	Expels darkness
Penetrates	Causes one to *see*
Extends brightness	Radiates
Projects	Reveals

The *workplace* is defined as a place where people are employed; the work setting in general. As a tenured employee of the federal government that spans across the three stages of my work life, I have experienced the number one problem that all federal employees face: *Bureaucracy*. As a manager and director/executive within corporate America, I have experienced the number one problem that all corporate employees face: *An inability to effectively communicate*. But, I have survived by often thinking about and reciting one of my favorite spiritual songs: *"When I think of the goodness of Jesus and all He's done for me, My soul cries out Halleluah, I thank God for saving me!"*

God has equipped each of His children with gifts that are unique and distinguishable from everyone else on earth. His Word says, *"Every good gift and every perfect gift is from above, and cometh down from the Father of **lights**, with whom is no variableness, neither shadow of turning"* (James 1:17). These gifts are without repentance. Further, God assures us in His Word that (KJV, emphasized):

He cannot change—*For I am the Lord, I change not* (Malachi 3:6);

He cannot lie—*That by two immutable things, in which it was impossible for God to lie* (Hebrews 6:18) and *In hope of eternal life, which God, that cannot lie, promised before the world began* (Titus 1:2);

He is the same forever—*Jesus Christ the same yesterday, and today, and forever* (Hebrews 13:8);

He cannot speak empty words—*So shall my word be that goeth forth out of my mouth: it shall not return unto me void, but it shall prosper in the things whereto I sent it* (Isaiah 55:11); and

He cannot break any promises—*My covenant will I not break, nor alter the thing that is gone out of my lips* (Psalm 89:34).

This *Workbook* is systemically divided into three parts:

Part One—*The formative years* is intended to remind the mature worker of our *humble beginnings* in our respective careers. It will also encourage those entering the workplace to focus on the important things and to dismiss the unimportant. I still remember my first day at work on July 23, 1984, exactly one week after my twenty-fourth birthday, at the Defense Personnel Support Center in Philadelphia, Pennsylvania. I vividly remember my first supervisors—Mr. Delma Hughes and Mrs. Catherine Ward—as I began my classroom and on-the-job training assignments in an old government warehouse equipped with third-hand furniture that was purchased at a General Services Administration auction. There was no air conditioning to cool the stifling Philadelphia heat that permeated the setting where I worked. For years, I sent Mrs. Ward a Christmas card as a sign of appreciation for showing her *light* in the midst of less than ideal working conditions. As we enter the workplace and transition *from growth to development to maturity*, we look to peers, supervisors, and other mentors to give us advice on how to advance to the next level. Mr. Hughes and Mrs. Ward, thank you.

Part Two—*The journeyman years* targets the group of workers who have learned and mastered the basic elements of the job and seek advancement into mid-level positions. During this phase, we tend to view our position as more than just a job, but a career. We find ourselves being asked to mentor others at the entry-level while, at the same time, earnestly seek senior-level officials to assist us with our next career move. Intelligence, tact, savvy, professionalism, integrity, balance, ethics, responsibility, and accountability are the key elements to succeed at this level. It is during this stage that we transition from learning to leading. It takes more than just the inner drive to succeed, it is also reliance upon the people that God places in our paths to lead, guide, and direct us. These are people whose trust we have earned through excellence and demonstrated potential on various projects over an extended period of time. They are those who will give us just enough room to make mistakes, yet protect us from their less passionate peers who salivate at the opportunity to openly humiliate their subordinates for the slightest of errors that have been committed. God placed wonderful people in my path in 1993 who were instrumental in launching my career development into the executive ranks. They too, are on my Christmas mailing list as a means to express my continued love for their protection and to keep them apprised of my family development and overall wellness. Formal leadership training reinforces the principle of application and self-motivation so that we will encourage others to reach their potential. Jesus taught His first disciples to *"launch out into the deep"* (Luke 5:4) and trust in His Word. In doing so, the fisher men, soon to be His disciples, let down their nets and caught so many fish that their nets broke (Luke 5:6)!

Part Three—*The mentoring years* encourages us to reinvest time and energy into people. People are the human capital of any organization and the most valuable asset in the workplace. A brief look at the lives of notable historians such as Evangelist Billy Graham and Dr. Martin Luther King, Jr. are inspirational stories of how two men, raised in the southern part of the United States of America, taught the world about the importance and awesome responsibility of raising the level of productivity of others. In the book of Genesis, chapter 1 and verse 28, God blesses man—male and female—after creating them in His image and after His likeness. God then gave four instructions and said unto them, *"Be fruitful, multiply, and replenish the earth, and subdue it."* Through the lives of Evangelist Graham and Dr. King, we have vivid examples on how to raise the level of productivity of others, as God instructs us.

Caution: *"For the love of money is the root of all evil"* (1 Timothy 6:10). Corporations thrive on their ability to make money and lots of it! In an era of antitrust, accounting irregularities, countless lawsuits, constant restructuring, employee layoffs, and outlandish bonuses to top executives, God can and will send a stern warning *"to humble ourselves under the mighty hand of God, that he may exalt you in due time"* (1 Peter 5:6) and *"Humble yourselves in the sight of the Lord, and he shall lift you up"* (James 4:10). In the book of Ephesians, Chapter 5, the Apostle Paul challenges and encourages the saints at Ephesus to walk as children of *light*. He begins in chapter 1, reminding them that our Heavenly Father has blessed them with all spiritual blessings in heavenly places in Christ (verse 3) and that He has chosen them before the foundation of the world that they should be holy and without blame before Him in love (verse 4). We have the same covenant right and God is speaking to us today. We are to be followers of God as dear children and walk in love, as Christ loved us (chapter 5, verses 1 and 2). Throughout chapter 5, Paul was inspired by God to write His instructions: *"For ye were sometimes darkness, but now are ye **light** in the Lord: walk as children of **light**"* (verse 8). *"And have no fellowship with the unfruitful works of darkness, but rather reprove them"* (verse 11). *"But all things that are reproved are made manifest by the light: for whatsoever doth make manifest is light. Wherefore he saith, AWAKE THOU THAT SLEEPEST, AND ARISE FROM THE DEAD, AND CHRIST SHALL GIVE THEE LIGHT"* (verses 13 and 14, emphasis added).

I intend to encourage all readers of this workbook with the comfort of God's Word. As things around us change all of the time, God remains the same: *"I am the LORD thy God and I change not"*

(Malachi 3:6). His Word shall stand forever (Isaiah 40:8). God loves you richly and desires the best for you. You are called to be *light* in the midst of darkness. Each of us have important responsibilities at work that transcends our daily tasks—and chances are they are not listed on any of our job descriptions.

A Candle Loses Nothing by Lighting Another Candle

Bear (endure, carry) one another's burdens and [a]troublesome moral faults, and in this way fulfill and observe perfectly the law of Christ (the Messiah) and complete [b]what is lacking [in your obedience to it].

—Galatians 6:2 AMP

Bear ye one another's burdens, and so fulfil the law of Christ.

—Galatians 6:2 KJV

The <u>Workplace</u> is Defined[1] as:

- *... a <u>place</u> (as a shop or factory) where work is done.*

- *... a person's place of employment.*

- *... any or all places where people are employed.*

[1] *The Merriam-Webster Unabridged Dictionary*

Student

Athlete

Singer

Executive Assistant

Artist

Laborer

Mechanic

Intern

Trainee

Office Manager

PART ONE

The Formative Years ... In the beginning

*Then God said, Let there be light, and there was **light**. God saw that the light was good, so he divided the **light** from the darkness.*

—Genesis 1:3–4 NCV

*And God said, Let there be light, and there was **light**. And God saw the light, that it was good: and God divided the **light** from the darkness.*

—Genesis 1:3–4 KJV

$\mathcal{T}$he formative years represent a period for growth, development, and maturity. God is a God of order (1 Corinthians 14:40) and these three beginning phases in the workplace are progressional—that is, they build one upon the other. Growth, development, and maturity are a time for new beginnings as it relates to life experiences, development of character, skills, knowledge, and abilities, and becoming a mature, responsible worker. Responsibility breeds accountability and visibility and *"to whom much is given, much is required"* (Luke 12:48).

As it relates to the workplace, *growth* is the phase when we learn to adapt to the environment where God has placed us. The workplace can be compared to a community that functions at its best when people choose to work well together and are genuinely kind to one another. In reality, very few offices function at their best due to the sinful nature of man. God's commandment to do unto others as we would have them to do unto us ("The Golden Rule"—Matthew 7:12) is rarely, if ever, actualized. What is desperately needed in the workplace is for God's chosen ones to be the *light* that will remind our co-workers about the enthusiasm they had when we they first gainfully employed, to remind them of the dreams that they had but have since lost along their respective journeys.

The *development* of one's skills, abilities, talents, and knowledge is self-initiated as we strive for excellence in our chosen career field. Hard work, practice at what we do, a desire to become the best in our chosen professions, accepting risky assignments, willingness to travel, and moving out of our comfort zone are positive steps to strengthen ourselves and demonstrate a passion to go beyond the call of duty. Be *light* to others as you develop your skills for a fruitful future in your chosen career field. Exemplify excellence in character, integrity, reliability, and workmanship throughout your entire workday. Be the spark that encourages your co-workers to develop their skills and motivate them to follow their dreams.

Maturity is the end result of the growth and development phases. The mature worker accepts responsibly for actions taken and for career progression. In the beginning of God's recorded Word, it is written, *"And God said, Let there be light, and there was light. And God saw the light, that it was good: and God divided the light from the darkness* (Genesis 1:3–4 KJV)." Light created organization where there once was chaos, then it dispelled darkness where it was once void (Genesis 1:2). This happened in the beginning before God planted seed that brought forth vegetation (Genesis 1:11). The seeds that we plant into our respective careers will produce fruit in our lives, and equally important, in the lives of others. Let your *light* so shine and your maturity illuminate in the workplace! Cause others to have a desire to achieve results that are visible as a result of your mature approach to office situations and circumstances.

Chapter One

Growth

"The office is a community, and like other communities, it functions best when people are polite and kind to one another. This means being polite to people at every level of the office hierarchy, not just those who are higher up."

—*Complete Book of Etiquette*, Amy Vanderbilt, 1952

So then, rid yourselves of all evil, all lying, hypocrisy, jealousy, and evil speech. As newborn babies want milk, you should want the pure and simple teaching. By it you can mature in your salvation, because you have already examined and seen how good the Lord is.

—1 Peter 2:1–3 NCV

Wherefore laying aside all malice, and all guile, and hypocrisies, and envies, and all evil speakings, as newborn babes, desire the milk of the word, that ye may grow thereby: If so be ye have tasted that the Lord is gracious.

—1 Peter 2:1–3 KJV

Be open to learn and grow.

*I*t is your first day at work. Perhaps fond memories bring a smile to your face. Perhaps they do not. It is a privilege to be gainfully employed and I view my first day on the job like the day that I accepted Jesus Christ as my personal Lord and Saviour. It is a day that I chose not to forget. It represents a new beginning. A transition from one state to another state—from unemployed to gainfully employed in a secure job. A positive change and new outlook on life is looking back at me when I look in the mirror.

One year earlier, 1983 to be exact, I had completed my undergraduate studies and desperately wanted to work. At this time in history, the United States was deep into an economic depression under the Reagan Administration. Finding gainful employment for a recent college graduate without relevant work experience can be a daunting task. Finally, my day arrived. Having just celebrated my twenty-fourth birthday one week earlier, my first day at work was on July 23, 1984, at the Defense Personnel Support Center in Philadelphia, Pennsylvania. It is still a vivid memory that I cherish. I was passionate and eager to learn and *grow*. I was ready to prove that I belonged and ready to apply what I had learned in college. I was ready to begin what I felt would be a productive career in the field of government contract negotiations and management. I liken it to a seed that had just been planted and more than eager to grow up to stand as tall and strong as an oak tree when it is fully mature.

Growth is a key barometer to success in the workplace. It is during this phase of one's career that the work environment will play a critical role in the growth of the worker. It is said, "The elevator to success is out of order. You'll have to use the stairs … one step at a time." In 1 Peter 2:1–3, the Apostle Peter teaches a profound message of growth:

> *Wherefore laying aside all malice, and all guile, and hypocrisies, and envies, and all evil speakings, As newborn babes, desire the sincere milk of the word, that ye may* ***grow thereby****: If so be ye have tasted that the Lord is gracious.*

—KJV

> *So clean house! Make a clean sweep of malice and pretense, envy and hurtful talk. You've had a taste of God. Now, like infants at the breast, drink deep of God's pure kindness. Then you'll grow up mature and whole in God.*

—The Message (MSG)

This is a message of growth from a disciple of Jesus Christ. Persecution can cause either growth or bitterness in the Christian life. The basic theme of this workbook is a proper response to Christian suffering. Peter knew that when the Christian stands for truth, justice, and fairness, they would need encouraging words to prepare them for the trials that would come. When we stand for truth in the workplace, persecution shall come. Peter writes this letter to give the Jewish believers a divine perspective on such trials so that they will be able and equipped to endure them without wavering in their faith.

For starters, view your fresh start as a new opportunity to learn, *grow*, and change. Twelve men were selected by Jesus Christ to carry out His mandate, *"to seek and to save that which was lost"* (Luke 19:10) after His death. His disciples received instructions, guidance, and counseling, for three and one-half years. A disciple is a learner, student, follower, and apprentice. It implies acceptance of the teacher's teachings and imitation of His practices (Luke 6:40 and Isaiah 8:16). Jesus' followers were called disciples (Luke 22:29), as are all Christians (Luke 14:26–27 and Acts 9:36). Part of their growth process was for some to abandon their current professions as fishermen (Simon Peter, Andrew, James [son of Zebedee], and John); a tax collector (Matthew); and other lines of work (Philip, Bartholomew, Thomas, James [son of Alphaeus], Thaddaeus, Simon [the Zealot], and Judas Iscariot, and follow Jesus. Jesus was their teacher, mentor, advisor, counselor, confidant, and protector. As followers and eyewitnesses, they observed His actions and obeyed His teachings, while taking heed to His consistent nature. Their leader was not a hypocrite, so the followers were open to grow and learn. The Apostle Peter's message of *growth* is extracted from what he learned from Jesus. During this time in biblical history, Christians were savagely treated in Rome, and this policy was probably reflected throughout the empire. Also, Christians were found throughout Asia Minor (currently the Republic of Turkey), as stated in 1 Peter chapter one, verse one. Christianity had not yet been received the official Roman ban, but the stage was being set for the persecution and martyrdom of the near future.

In the book of Romans, the Apostle Paul writes a comforting message of encouragement to the saints at Rome. Paul's writings mirror his gift of exhortation and are overwhelmingly encouraging to his intended audience. During his conversion from King Saul on Damascus Road, he had a conversation with Jesus. Although he was not a disciple of Jesus, Paul bears the title of an apostle because of his personal encounter with Jesus on Damascus Road (Acts 9:4–6).

> *For by the grace (unmerited favor of God) given to me I warn everyone among you not to estimate and think of himself more highly than he ought [not to have an exaggerated opinion of his own importance], but to rate his ability with sober judgment, each according to the degree of faith apportioned by God to him.*

—Romans 12:3 AMP

> *For I say, through the grace given unto me, to every man that is among you, not to think of himself more highly than he ought to think; but to think soberly, according as God hath dealt to every man the measure of faith.*

—Romans 12:3 KJV

Considered his greatest work, Paul's message of *growth* focuses on our responsibilities to God. First, we are to:

- Recognize that we must offer our bodies a living sacrifice.
- Live a holy lifestyle that is acceptable unto God.
- Eliminate the cursing, bad attitude, backbiting, lying, and whatever does not represent God favorably.

That is our reasonable service, or the least that we can do. Next, we are *not* to

- Be conformed to this world in carrying out His mandate.
- Follow man's lustful desires for fame, fortune, and prestige.

Instead, we are to renew our mind with the Word of God and in accordance to His will. In doing so, we demonstrate to the world and prove what is good and acceptable.

Lastly, we are to think soberly, and not be puffed up, according to the measure of faith that God has dealt to each of us. To be high-minded means to put self before others. That does not produce growth, but stagnates it.

Placed first among his thirteen epistles in the New Testament, this book explores the significance of Jesus' sacrificial death. Using a question-and-answer format, Paul records the most systematic presentation of doctrine in *The Holy Bible*. It is a book of practical exhortation and encouragement. Key words such as righteousness, faith, law, all, and sin each appear at least sixty times in this book.

NOTES:

_____

_____

_____

_____

Planning Your Life to be a Winner

Have you ever heard this phrase: If you fail to plan, you have, in essence, planned to fail? Therefore, consider the below statements during this phase of your career for future planning purposes.

1. We owe it to ourselves to bring out the best of who we are—to use our talents for something beautiful—and worthy. That requires a staying power that comes only with vision and determination.

2. You need a plan to become what the Lord wants you to be. Here are the essential steps:
   a) Have a vision/dream;
   b) Get the facts and be aware of what is going on around you;
   c) Analyze your strengths and weaknesses;
   d) Make a few assumptions;
   e) Set definite measurable objectives;

f) Be in a state of continual prayer (God will confirm, through the Holy Spirit, what is right for you);

g) Develop a list of strategies for each objective;

h) Put the plan into action;

i) Review progress; and

j) Reward yourself for accomplishment.

3. The difference between winning and losing in our lives can be measured by the margin. Whenever the marginal play comes along, you will excel, and in the process, become all that you can be.

4. The difference between the winner of the PGA Golf Tournament and the tenth player is an average of one stroke, the fiftieth player only four strokes. You have to be a really good golfer to even be in the top 200, but a margin of only six strokes separates the top from the two hundredth player.

5. In a study of aerodynamics, one learns that the leading portion of the wing provides most of an airplane's lift. Of all of the square feet of space on the plane, only this very small area up and down each wing provides the margin to lift the plane.

Source: Migliore, R. Henry, *Dare to Succeed: A Treasury of Inspiration and Wisdom for Life and Career*, Honor Books: 1994.

In his book, *Managing God's Time*, author Michel A. Bell identifies four key factors to evaluate before committing to decisions. It is the second quadrant of the P-Squares that is titled *Priorities*:

God	**Work**
Family	**Relationships**

Priorities help establish the relative importance of activities and relationship in the process of achieving our objectives. They determine the likely effects of accepting and performing an event based on existing commitments, future activities, and most importantly, on our various types of relationships.

Understanding in advance the likely implications of a new assignment or task on existing projects and relationships does the following:

- Encourages preemptive discussions about delivery of specific projects with relevant persons in order to eliminate unwanted "surprises."

- Allows the mitigation or elimination of adverse consequences on existing projects and relationships.

- Helps to improve our daily effectiveness by emphasizing the important rather than the urgent. Hence, examining our priorities first:

- We emphasize projects based on our overall goals.
- We *nurture significant relationships* irrespective of how many projects we are required to complete.

I propose putting four key priorities in place:
1. First: God (Matthew 6:33)
2. Second: Family (Ephesians 5:22–6:4)
3. Third: Work (Colossians 3:23)
4. Fourth: Relationships (Proverbs 27:17)

Our Valued Asset in the Workplace

The growth of the personal computer (PC) is perhaps one of the most historic events in world history. In 2012, these indisputable facts were published to support this claim:

- Internet traffic is projected to quadruple between 2012 and 2016.
- China has over one million mobile phone users.
- The top ten in-demand jobs in 2010 did not exist in 2004.
- The average American spends twenty-four hours, or one entire day each week, online.
- One-third of U.S. adults say they would not be able to live without the Internet.
- Ninety-five percent of U.S. teens are online.
- Terrorist groups are active on 4,000 websites.
- Nearly one-fifth of Windows PCs in the U.S. lack any security protection.
- The U.S. Government needs to hire at least 10,000 cyber security experts.
- The private sector needs to hire at least four times that amount, or 40,000 cyber security experts.

Evolution Of the p c

Fifty years ago this moment, a computerpioneer said, "There is no reason to suppose the average boy or girl cannot be master of a personal computer." Soon after, PC's arrived - and now grownup boys and girls cannot imagine our lives without them.

By Betsy Towner

PDP - 8

ATARI

APPLE 1

PET

CCMPASS

1962 The LINC (Laboratory Instrument Computer) begins processing data in an MIT lab to assist with biomecical research. The minicomputer paves the way for PCs.

1965 The PDP-8, made by Digital Equipment Corp., debuts and becomes the first minicomputer success Price: $18,000

1969 The Department of Defenseestablishes the first computer network, called the ARPRAnet - later named the internet.

1971 ARPAnet transmits the first email.

1972 Atari releases Pong, kick starting the video game industry.

1975 *Popular Electronics* puts the Altair 8800 Computer kit on it's January cover, and it's maker, MITS is flooded with orders. Memory: 256 bytes.

1977 The Commodore PET, Apple I and Tandy Radio Shack's TRS-80 all debut.

1981 IBM calls its mini computer the PC, turning the descripyion into a brand. Sales soar

Then Now

	Then	Now
	1962 LINC	2012 iPhone
	about 8 square foot	5 x 2 inches
	1kb of memory (1,000 bytes)	16 gb of memory (16,000,000,000 bytes)
	sold for $43,000	**sold for** $199

1982 Grid Systems releases Compass, the first laptop. Price: $8,150. •*Time* names the computer "Machine of the Year" in a story written on a typewriter.

1983 Compaq Computer Corp. makes the first PC clone, 100% compatible with IBM's PC. First-year sales: $111million

1984 Apple Machintosh debuts during a $1.5 million Super Bowl commercial. The Mac is the first successful computer to feature a mouse and user friendly graphics.

1990 The World Wide Web is invented. •The first successful version of Microsoftt's Windows 3.0 launches.

1995 Amazon and Ebay both debut, revolutionizing the way we shop.

1998 Google and PayPal both debut, transforming information searches and financial transactions. ● Apple's successful iMac becomes the first in it's line of Products.

2007 Apple's iPhone goes on sale, boasting up to 8 gigabytes of memory in a pocket-size phone

2008 Apple launches the iPad, selling more than 3000,000 on the tablet's debut day.

2012 iPhone 5 debuts.

SOURCES: COMPUTER HISTORY.GLOBEUALHISTORY.COM NATIONAL INSTITUTE OF HEALTH.COLDGOMPUTERS.AND SAFETYHOWARE.COM NEW YORK TIMES

Source: AARP Magazine, November 2012.

Three Phases of Growth

Growth is a process that happens over time. It never stops. The workplace is an environment that changes virtually every day. Our ability, or inability, to be flexible to these changes either propels or stifles our personal growth. This process of growth, according the Word of God, involves two meaningful steps: (1) A correct attitude that is required to promote growth, and humility; and (2) Be ever mindful of the small beginnings. This process is expressly recorded in *The Holy Bible* as a guide for us to follow, apply, and live by. Like the seed that is a small source of life, as it is planted into good ground, it grows to a mature state over time. It reproduces after its own kind (Genesis 1:11–12).

Grow(th), in the original Greek language, has three meanings:

1. *Auxanō*—"to *grow* or increase," of the growth of that which lives, naturally or spiritually.
2. *Auxēsis*—"increase"—Ephesians 4:16; Colossians 2:19.
3. *Huperauxanō* —"to increase beyond measure," is used of faith and love, in their living and practical effects (2 Thessalonians 1:3).

Auxēsis

From him the whole body, joined and held together by every supporting ligament, grows and builds itself up in love, as each part does its work.

—Ephesians 4:16 NIV

From whom the whole body fitly joined together and compacted by that which every joint supplieth, according to the effectual working in the measure of every part, maketh increase of the body unto the edifying of itself in love.

—Ephesians 4:16 KJV

God created man in His image and after His likeness (Genesis 1:26). Further, man is fearfully and wonderfully made (Psalm 139:14) and even the very hairs on our head are all numbered (Matthew 10:30). God designed our body parts to work together in unison so that we can function at our optimum levels. The more cohesive the group, the better it works together. Similarly, we are supposed to *grow* together as a cohesive work group on the job without giving preference to one over another. Then, God gives the increase. As God unites Christians with Himself, Christ also brings them into a harmonious relationship with one another. This harmony is accomplished *by that which every joint supplieth*. The spiritual gifts mentioned in verses 7 through 15 are figuratively likened to the various "joints" or "ligaments" of the body. Christ joins believers together and unites them by the divinely ordained ministries of Christians who possess diverse spiritual gifts, which are exercised and used among believers for the common good—even at work. As such, the productivity of everyone involved increases.

And not holding the Head, from which all the body of joints and bands having nourishment ministered, and knit together, increaseth with the increase of God.

—Colossians 2:19 KJV

And they are not connected to Christ, the head of the body. For he holds the whole body together with its joints and ligaments, and it grows as God nourishes it.

—Colossians 2:19 New Living Translation (NLT)

Working together, while acknowledging your role on the team, is what makes the whole team cohesive, dynamic, and creative. The Greek word *holding* means to hold fast to someone as to remain united with Christ (Head). *Having nourishment ministered, and knit together* means being supported and united. From Christ (Head), then, the church (body) derives spiritual growth as it is supported and united by the various ministering believers (joints). In doing so, we increase in Him and can be the *light* that is so desperately needed in the workplace.

Huperauxanō

With love as the motivating factor, you cannot fail. Because love never fails.

We are bound to thank God always for you, brethren, as it is meet, because that your faith groweth exceedingly, and the charity of every one of you all toward each other aboundeth.

—2 Thessalonians 1:3 KJV

Dear brothers and sisters,[a] we can't help but thank God for you, because your faith is flourishing and your love for one another is growing.

—2 Thessalonians 1:3 NLV

The Apostle Paul again expresses his pleasure with the spiritual growth of the intended audience. His earlier fears have been dispelled based upon the testimony of the Thessalonians. This book is Paul's second letter to them in response to certain reports, from Timothy, that had come concerning their progress. What is significant about Paul's message is that he saw such potential in this little church to the north that he established on his second missionary journey. During Paul's day, Thessalonica was the capital of Macedonia. His ministry in the city lasted only one month, yet this city became famous for its wealth as well as its attraction of a strange mixture of Roman high society and pagan sensuality. This influx of cultural diversities created confusion and conflicting beliefs about Jesus Christ. However, this small church's love and faith caused *growth* beyond measure because it was founded on Paul's steadfast love of Christ.

NOTES:

_____

_____

_____

_____

A Correct Attitude to Grow

Your attitude is one of the few things that is completely under your control. Life is 10% of what happens to us, yet 90% of how we respond to life's situations and circumstances. Jesus Christ's first public sermon is a powerful teaching about the importance of having a correct attitude. His timing is crucial as He teaches this awesome message after being tempted by Satan on three different occasions. In Matthew, chapter four, *The Holy Bible* records the confrontation between Jesus and Satan. Jesus had fasted for forty days and forty nights and was hungry (verse 2). Satan attempted to persuade Jesus to "partner" with him during this trying time. He mistakenly assumed that Jesus was too weak to resist his three proposals. But, the Word records their conversations as follows (emphasis added):

> *If thou be the Son of God, command that these stones be made bread. But He answered and said, It is written, MAN SHALL NOT LIVE BY BREAD ALONE, BUT BY EVERY WORD THAT PROCEEDETH OUT OF THE MOUTH OF GOD. Then the devil taketh Him up into the holy city, and setteth Him on a pinnacle of the temple. And said unto Him, If thou be the Son of God, cast thyself down ... Jesus said unto him, It is written again, THOU SHALL NO TEMPT THE LORD THY GOD. Again, the devil took Him up into an exceeding high mountain, and shewed Him all the kingdoms of this world, and the glory of them; And said unto Him, All these things I will give thee, if thou fall down and worship me. Then Jesus said unto him, Get thee hence, Satan: for it is written, THOU SHALL WORSHIP THE LORD THY GOD, AND HIM ONLY SHALT THOU SERVE.*

—Matthew 4:4–10 KJV

> *Jesus answered, "It is written: 'Man shall not live on bread alone, but on every word that comes from the mouth of God.'[b] "5 Then the devil took him to the holy city and had him stand on the highest point of the temple. 6 "If you are the Son of God," he said, "throw yourself down. For it is written: 'He will command his angels concerning you, and they will lift you up in their hands, so that you will not strike your foot against a stone.'[b] "7 Jesus answered him, "It is also written: 'Do not put the Lord your God to the test.'[c] "8 Again, the devil took him to a very high mountain and showed him all the kingdoms of the world and their splendor. 9 "All this I will give you," he said, "if you will bow down and worship me."10 Jesus said to him, "Away from me, Satan! For it is written: 'Worship the Lord your God, and serve him only.'[d] "*

—Matthew 4:4–10 NIV

Then the devil leaveth Him, and, behold, angels came and ministered unto Him (verse 11).

The Beatitudes—*the attitude we ought to be*—is the first message that Jesus taught in His Sermon on the Mount as recorded in Matthew, chapter 5, verses one through twelve:

And seeing the multitudes, He went up into a mountain: and when he was set, His disciples came unto Him: And He opened His mouth, and taught them, saying,

:3   *Blessed are the poor in spirit: for theirs is the kingdom of heaven.*   —KJV

*God blesses those who are poor and realize their need for him, [a]
for the Kingdom of Heaven is theirs.*   —NLT

Attitude #1—Humility

:4   *Blessed are they that mourn, for they shall be comforted.*   —KJV

They are blessed who grieve, for God will comfort them.   —NCV

Attitude #2—Concern about the sinful condition of this world

:5   *Blessed are the meek: for they shall inherit the earth.*   —KJV

*You're blessed when you're content with just who you are—no more,
no less. That's the moment you find yourselves proud owners of everything
that can't be bought.*   —MSG

Attitude #3—Keep your strength (power) under control

:6   *Blessed are they which do hunger and thirst after righteousness:
for they shall be filled.*   —KJV

*Blessed are those who hunger and thirst for righteousness,
For they shall be filled.*   —New King James Version (NKJV)

Attitude #4—Fulfillment comes from being right with God

:7   *Blessed are the merciful: for they shall obtain mercy.*   —KJV

They are blessed who show mercy to others, for God will show mercy to them.   —NCV

Attitude #5—Be compassionate towards the plight of others

:8   *Blessed are the pure in heart: for they shall see God.*   —KJV

*Blessed (happy, [a] enviably fortunate, and [b] spiritually prosperous—
possessing the [c] happiness produced by the experience of God's favor and*

especially conditioned by the revelation of His grace, regardless of their outward conditions) are the pure in heart, for they shall see God! —AMP

Attitude #6—Be sincere in your actions

:9 *Blessed are the peacemakers: for they shall be called the children of God.* —KJV

You're blessed when you can show people how to cooperate instead of compete or fight. That's when you discover who you really are, and your place in God's family. —MSG

Attitude #7—Avoid strife, drama, and contentions. Exhibit a peaceful demeanor even in the midst of a storm

:10 *Blessed are they which are persecuted for righteousness' sake: for theirs is the kingdom of heaven.* —KJV

They are blessed who are persecuted for doing good, for the kingdom of heaven belongs to them. —NCV

Attitude #8—Others will not understand that your success is contingent upon your Godly lifestyle and your personal relationship with God, through Jesus Christ. When they resent it and speak evil against you, continue to seek God first and foremost in everything

:11 *Blessed are ye, when men shall revile you, and persecute you, and shall say all manner of evil against you falsely, for my sake.* —KJV

Blessed are you when people insult you, persecute you and falsely say all kinds of evil against you because of me. —NIV

Attitude #9—Remain steadfast in the faith. Even Jesus was persecuted

:12 *Rejoice, and be exceeding glad: for great is your reward in heaven: for so persecuted they the prophets which were before you.* —KJV

Be glad and supremely joyful, for your reward in heaven is great (strong and intense), for in this same way people persecuted the prophets who were before you. —AMP

A positive attitude is a powerful force. It cannot be stopped!

NOTES:

_____

_____

_____

_____

Do Not Despise the Small Beginnings

Everything *big* starts with something *small*. A mustard seed is so small that it is difficult to see. However, when it grows to full maturity, it is one of the largest plants on the face of the earth. Under favorable conditions, its dimensions, after fully mature, can be ten to twelve feet tall after only five months!

Who [with reason] despises the day of small things? For these seven shall rejoice when they see the plummet in the hand of Zerubbabel. [These seven] are the eyes of the Lord which run to and fro throughout the whole earth.

—Zechariah 4:10 AMP

For who hath despised the day of small things? For they shall rejoice, and shall see the plummet of the hand of Zerubbabel with those seven; they are the eyes of the Lord, which run to and fro through the whole earth.

—Zechariah 4:10 KJV

One kernel of corn can produce a stalk with two ears, each having 200 kernels. From those 400 kernels come 400 more stalks, producing 160,000 kernels. From those 160,000 kernels, come 160,000 more stalks, producing a total of 64 million kernels. The principle of compounding is at work here.[2]

Dr. Polly Matzinger was working as a cocktail waitress when she was "discovered" to be a scientist in the making. Today, some think her theory about the immune system could revolutionize the way we treat disease. For decades, scientists thought that the immune system reacts to foreign cells entering the body. Instead, Dr. Matzinger postulates that the system responds only when it receives signals from injured cells. "Think of the body as a community that welcomes visitors," she says, "but alerts the cops when someone starts breaking windows. In the same way, the immune system is alerted by damage-induced alarm signals, not foreign cells." The Danger Model challenges the theory on how the body defends itself. Dr. Matzinger, now section head of the National Institute of Allergy and Infectious Diseases in Bethesda, Maryland, began in an unrelated field of endeavor. This college dropout, dog trainer, jazz musician, carpenter, and waitress, found each of her jobs boring. It was through conversations with faculty members that frequented the bar that she interjected her knowledge about evolutionary adaptations in skunks that got the attention of the faculty. She was then encouraged to become scientist and completed her field of study by earning a Ph.D. from the University of California at San Diego. "What's nice about science is if things don't make sense, you can question them and not get fired for it," she commented.[3]

Walk worthy in the job that you have:

---

[2] Gass, Bob, "Word for Today," April 30, 2002.
[3] Ryan, Michael, "She's Not Afraid to Ask Questions", *Parade Magazine*, March 24, 2002.

I therefore, the prisoner of the Lord, beseech you that ye walk worthy of the vocation wherewith ye are called.

—Ephesians 4:1 KJV

I therefore, the prisoner for the Lord, appeal to and beg you to walk (lead a life) worthy of the [divine] calling to which you have been called [with behavior that is a credit to the summons to God's service.

—Ephesians 4:1 AMP

Your walk should reflect your calling. Bring credit to His name every day. God doesn't call the qualified, He qualifies the called. Live in a manner befitting the divine call that summoned you to salvation.

Recognizing and acknowledging the three phases of growth, having a proper attitude aligned with the will of God, excelling in your role, and having basic workplace manners will assist you to develop the foundational skills necessary to successfully compete on the job. Seek first the Kingdom, and His righteousness, and God will provide you with the "things" that you need to sustain you (Matthew 6:33).

Prioritize Your Time

Did you know that in the United Kingdom (UK), Health and Safety Executive's commissioned research revealed the following data?

- Up to 500,000 people experience work-related stress at a level they believe is making them ill
- Up to five million people in the UK feel "very" or "extremely" stressed by their work
- Work-related stress costs society between £3.7 billion and £3.8 billion every year (based upon 1995/1996 prices)

To avoid this dilemma in the midst of your *growth* phase in the workplace, consider your Personal Time Inventory in the management of your precious time.

Personal Time Inventory Summary (PTI)

Activities	**Actual**: Hours Spent in a Typical 24-hour Day	**Goal**: Hours Spent in a Typical 24-hour Day
Sleep		
Meals and Personal Care		
Work		
God		
Commute		
Telephone		

Internet		
Television		
Housework		
Spouse and Children		
My Time		
Sports		
Other		

Source: Bell, Michel A. *Managing God's Time: Personal Effectiveness Improvement*, WinePress Publishing, 2004

food for thought

ON GROWTH

God's Photo Album

In a book entitled, *God's Photo Album*, by Shelly Mecum and the children and families of Our Lady of Perpetual Help School, rests an inspirational story about how they looked for God and saved their school. Ms. Mecum and her students had a dream, and the courage and faith, to make their dream soar. Determined to save the struggling Ewa Beach Elementary School on Oahu, Hawaii, they mobilized an entire community to realize her vision: a spiritual quest for God and a brave book-writing adventure. Some 168 young children and their families, ranging from five to eighty years old, toted cameras, notebooks, and pencils across the island by bus, trolley, and glass-bottom boat. Their mission? To find **God.** Enclosed throughout the pages of this wonderful book are snapshots and inspiring observations offering unforgettable moments of grace. Proof that no dream is too big!

Questions for Personal Reflection or Group Discussion

1. Time management is a challenging task. What steps, if any, are you taking to ensure that your time is spent wisely?

   _____

   _____

   _____

2. How is your attitude based upon Jesus' teaching in Matthew, chapter 5?

   _____

   _____

   _____

3. Growth is a continual process that impacts our lives based upon our choice. What choices are you making?

   _____

   _____

   _____

4. Have you grown in your Christian walk? Cite some examples.

   _____

   _____

   _____

5. What specific experience can you remember that caused growth in your life?

   _____

   _____

   _____

Chapter Two

Development

"I've missed more than 9,000 shots in my career,
I've lost almost 300 games,
26 times, I've been trusted to take the game winning shot,
and missed.
I've FAILED over and over
and over again in my life.
And that is why
I SUCCEED."

—Michael Jordan, 1997 Nike ad reflecting on the career of
the world's greatest professional basketball player.

The teaching of your word gives light, so even the simple can understand.

—Psalm 119:130 NLT

*The entrance of thy words giveth **light**; it giveth understanding unto the simple.*

—Psalm 119:130 KJV

Develop skills along the way. Never stop learning.

$\mathscr{F}$ew would argue that the best basketball player ever in the National Basketball Association (NBA) is Michael Jordan. His career statistics, prior to his second and third retirement from the game, speak for themselves:

Stat	Event/Accomplishment
2	Olympic gold medals (1984 and 1992)
3	NBA All-Star Game Most Valuable Player (1988, 1996, 1998)
5	NBA regular season MVPs (1988, 1991, 1992, 1996, 1998)
6	NBA Finals MVPs (NBA record)
9	NBA All-Defensive First Team selections (NBA record)
10	NBA scoring titles (NBA record)
21.3	All-star scoring average (NBA record)
26	Free throws made in 27 attempts versus the New Jersey Nets on February 26, 1987
31.5	Regular season scoring average
33.4	Playoff scoring average (NBA record)
35	Points scored in first half of 1992 NBA Finals Game 1 (NBA record)
41	Scoring average, 1993 NBA Finals versus the Phoenix Suns (NBA Finals record)
63	Points scored versus the Boston Celtics on April 20, 1986 (NBA Playoff record)
69	Points scored versus the Cleveland Cavaliers on March 28, 1990 (career high)
5,987	Playoff points scored (NBA record)
29,277	Regular season points scored

Source: Upper Deck Collectibles, 1999. Authenticated number 10,126 of 99,000 printed.

However, the initial rejection and an inability to earn a roster spot on the varsity basketball team in high school was the spark that lit his fire! The heart of this champion was revealed publicly, in April 1982, during the division I college basketball national championship game in Albuquerque, New Mexico: Georgetown University versus the University of North Carolina. As a college freshman, he helped his team win the game by having the courage to launch a fifteen-foot jump shot with only a few remaining seconds left in regulation. His team trailed by one point. As the ball left his hand, the capacity crowd of 15,000-plus cheering fans echoed the infamous chant: *WHOOOSH!* That sound is symbolic of knowing that the ball is going into the basket. Now, the University of North Carolina basketball team leads by one point. An unforced turnover by a Georgetown University guard seals the victory for the University of North Carolina.

At the professional level, Jordan *developed* his game throughout his career and ultimately led a struggling franchise in the city of Chicago to six NBA championships. This franchise defeated a different team each time. It began in the 1990–1991 season against the high flying Los Angeles Lakers and their star Earvin "Magic" Johnson. It ended in the 1997–1998 season against the fundamentally sound and precision-like Utah Jazz and their two stars, and NBA hall-of-famers, John Stockton and Karl Malone.

In the Inaugural SI 50: The Power Issue, *Sports Illustrated* magazine, March 11, 2013, Michael Jordan is listed as the fiftieth most influential figure in sports. As owner of the NBA's Charlotte Bobcats, his Q rating is 43; Peyton Manning, four-time National Football League Most Valuable Player, is next at 32. The Jordan Brand grew an estimated 25% in 2012, to $60 million, generating more in basketball shoes sales than the rest of Nike.

> *"The first and most important step toward success is the feeling that we can succeed."*
> —NELSON BOSWELL, AUTHOR

We are all faced with a series of great opportunities brilliantly disguised as impossible situations. In times of change, learners inherit the earth while the learned find themselves beautifully equipped to deal with a world that no longer exists.

Development (a noun) is defined as the act or process of developing. It also means *maturity*—a developed state or form. Develop (a verb) is defined as follows:

(1) To bring out the possibilities of; bring to a more advanced, effective, or usable state;

(2) To cause to grow or expand;

(3) To bring into being or activity; produce;

(4) To cause to mature or evolve; and

(5) To grow into a mature state; advance; expand.

In his book titled "*Strength Finder 2.0,*" Tom Rath identifies thirty-four themes and ideas for *action*. Based upon my reading and assessment of these ideas as it pertains to the workplace, three apply:

- Achiever—Your achiever theme helps explain your drive. Achiever describes a constant need for achievement. You feel as if every day starts at zero. By the end of the day you must achieve something tangible in order to feel good about yourself. And by "every day" you mean every single day—workdays, weekends, and vacations.

- Focus—"Where am I headed?" you ask yourself. You ask this question every day. Guided by this theme of focus, you need a clear destination. Lacking one, your life and your work can quickly become frustrating. And so each year, each month, and even each week you set goals. These goals serve as your compass, helping you determine priorities and make the necessary corrections to get back on course. Your focus is powerful because it forces you to filter; you instinctively evaluate whether or not a particular action will help you move toward your goal.

- Responsibility—Your responsibility theme forces you to take psychological ownership for anything you commit to, and whether large or small, you feel emotionally bound to follow it through to completion. Your good name depends on it. If for some reason you cannot deliver, you automatically start to look for ways to make it up to the other person. Apologies are not enough. Excuses and rationalizations are totally unacceptable. You will not be able to live with yourself until you have made restitution.

NOTES:

_____

_____

_____

_____

Connect to God (Mind and Body)

Your Mind

"Mind" is used ninety-five times in *The Holy Bible*. In the original Greek, *nous* means the seat of reflective consciousness, comprising the faculties of perception and understanding, and those of feeling, judging, and determining. The mind is the divine center of choice. Choices are long lasting and life changing. It is also where our thoughts reside. Thoughts become words, words become actions, actions become habits, our habits shape our character, and our character will determine our future.[4]

In the November 6, 2000, issue of *U.S. News and World Report*, an article entitled "How to Master the New Workplace, Career Guide 2001," the opening statement under the subtitle on page 56 is self-explanatory: "The new workplace is risky, rugged, and rewarding. And guess what? You're in charge!" The Apostle Paul, in his letter to the Romans, emphasizes that point as well. Our environment at work is risky, rugged, and rewarding, and we are in charge. Paul writes:

*Be ye not conformed to this world: but be ye transformed by the renewing of your **mind**, that ye may prove what is that good, and acceptable, and perfect will of God.*

—Romans 12:2 KJV

*Do not be shaped by this world; instead be changed within by a **new way of thinking**. Then you will be able to decide what God wants for you; you will know what is good and pleasing to him and what is perfect.*

—Romans 12:2 NCV

---

[4] Idleman, Shane. *Success Guide*, Issue 101, January, 2001.

We are to resist being poured into the mold of the present thinking, value systems, and conduct of this world. *"Be not conformed"* is only used again in 1 Peter 1:14.

With our minds, we can understand God's word, if we choose to. Understanding God's Word requires readiness and an act of our will (*attitude*). There are two words in the original Greek language that best describe using our minds to understand:

1. *Ginōskō*—to allow oneself to learn, and
2. *Manthanō*—to understand learning.

Used together, they have a tri-fold meaning:

1. To allow oneself to increase in knowledge,
2. To learn by use and practice, and
3. To allow understanding by an act of one's will.

The entrance of thy words giveth light; it giveth understanding unto the simple.

—Psalm 119:130 KJV

The unfolding of your words gives light; it gives understanding to the simple.

—Psalm 119:130 NIV

NOTES:

_____

_____

_____

_____

Your Body

The principle of isometrics is that you can build muscle by pushing firmly against an unyielding object. You can build character the same way (Phyllis Haxton).

This principle is true for the human body as well. "Body" is referenced 173 times in *The Holy Bible*. In the original Greek, *sōma* means the body as a whole, the instrument of life whether of man living (Matthew 6:22) or dead (Matthew 27:52). "Vessel," has various meanings in the context of the English language. Specifically, as it relates to the human body, it is defined as a person regarded as a holder or receiver of a particular trait or quality. In the original Greek, *skeuos*, means for the service of God (Acts 9:15), a chosen vessel (2 Timothy 2:21), an earthen vessel (2 Corinthians 4:7), the human frame (2 Corinthians 4:7 and 1 Thessalonians 4:4), and the subjects of divine mercy and wrath (Romans 9:22–23). It is used 193 times in *The Holy Bible* in both its singular and plural forms. We are vessels, used by God to carry out His will in the earth and on our respective jobs. For reasons He never explains,

He chooses to work through ordinary people like us. He placed us in situations that ultimately unlock our compassion and creativity. He connects us with people who can open doors that we are not equipped or knowledgeable about how to open. He makes us a solution for wherever we go. Forming a vessel is a lifelong process. If the potter does not continually wet the clay, it becomes too hard to be worked. Therefore, allow God to *shape* you into the vessel that He desires so that He can use you mightily!

> *So I went to the potter's house, and sure enough, the potter was there, working away at his wheel. Whenever the pot the potter was working on turned out badly, as sometimes happens when you are working with clay, the potter would simply start over and use the same clay to make another pot.*

> —Jeremiah 18:3–4 MSG

> *And the vessel that he made of clay was marred in the hand of the potter: so he made it again another vessel, as seemed good to the potter to make it.*

> —Jeremiah 18:4 KJV

We were bought with a price. Our "bodies" do not belong to us. The scriptures says, *"The EARTH is the LORD'S, and the fullness thereof, the world, and they that dwell therein"* (Psalm 24:1). Since we belong to Him, we are to use our bodies for His service. This is why the Lord repeatedly teaches us to flee from sexual sins. Sin requires us to use the body in a manner that is unfitting for kingdom use.

> *What? Know ye not that your body is the temple of the Holy Ghost which is in you, which ye have of God, and ye are not your own? For ye are bought with a price: therefore glorify God in your body, and in your spirit, which are God's.*

> —1 Corinthians 6:19–20 KJV

> *Or do you not know that your body is the temple of the Holy Spirit who is in you, whom you have from God, and you are not your own? [20] For you were bought at a price; therefore glorify God in your body[a] and in your spirit, which are God's.*

> —1 Corinthians 6:19–20 NKJV

The price paid was the blood of Jesus Christ (Acts 20:28). This has profound significance for the believer (1 Timothy 4:10 and 1 Peter 2:9) who has been called out of darkness into His marvelous light.

Develop Into Your Role

> *I am, just as you are, a unique, never-to-be-repeated event in this universe. Therefore, I have, just as you have, a unique, never-to-be-repeated role in this world.*

> —George Sheehan

Before you set goals, discover your God-ordained purpose. You have the ministry (*of reconciliation*) whether you know it or not. People are dying because they don't know what Jesus has done for them. The economy is no longer robust as it was under the Clinton Administration in the 1990s. Corporate executives are being openly punished and humiliated, as they should, for willful misconduct that negatively affects the lives of thousands of employees. Multi-billion dollar corporations are filing for bankruptcy protection as a means to save face while, at the same time, personal bankruptcy is at an all-time high. Police officers are still being videotaped abusing their authority. The value of family, based upon God's Word, has deteriorated to the extent of becoming less meaningful than one's desire to please their employer. The dot-com and telecommunications bubbles that once seemed impenetrable have burst. Many developing countries are wastelands of poverty, hunger, and disease. But, as faithful believers in Christ, we have the answer. Look at some of His benefits and provisions that He has for His chosen children:

Don't love money; be satisfied with what you have. For God has said, I will never fail you. I will never abandon you[a]

—Hebrews 13:5 NLT

Let your conversation be without covetousness; and be content with such things as ye have: for he hath said, I will never leave thee, nor forsake thee.

—Hebrews 13:5 KJV

Benefit/Provision #1—God's provisions are eternal

Behold, I give you power to tread on serpents and scorpions, and over all the power of the enemy: and nothing shall by any means hurt you.

—Luke 10:19 KJV

I have given you authority to walk all over snakes and scorpions. You will be able to destroy all the power of the enemy. Nothing will harm you.

—Luke 10:19 New International Reader's Version (NIRV)

Benefit/Provision #2—We have authority over spiritual wickedness in high places in the name of Jesus

The thief's purpose is to steal and kill and destroy. My purpose is to give them a rich and satisfying life.

—John 10:10 NLT

The thief cometh not, but for to steal, and to kill, and to destroy: I am come that they might have life, and that they might have it more abundantly.

—John 10:10 KJV

Benefit/Provision #3—We are no longer subject to the power of darkness but have been translated into the marvelous *light!* Satan no longer has authority over our lives

You will keep in perfect peace those whose minds are steadfast, because they trust in you.

—Isaiah 26:3 NIV

Thou wilt keep him in perfect peace, whose mind is stayed on thee: because he trusteth in thee.

—Isaiah 26:3 KJV

Benefit/Provision #4—Peace will keep you healthy and functional within the kingdom of God

There are so many awesome benefits and provisions in *The Holy Bible* that the Lord has provided for us. To know them, however, we must become intimately acquainted with Him and His holy Word. Otherwise, you could finish up somewhere you should not be or succeed at something God never called you to do.

Benefit/Provision #5—To lose is not always failure

This poor man cried, and the LORD heard him, and saved him out of all his troubles.

—Psalm 37:6 KJV

And He will make your uprightness and right standing with God go forth as the light, and your justice and right as [the shining sun of] the noonday.

—Psalm 37:6 AMP

Benefit/Provision #6—Knowing about God is fascinating; Knowing God personally is life changing

GOD's Message:

> *Don't let the wise brag of their wisdom. Don't let heroes brag of their exploits. Don't let the rich brag of their riches. If you brag, brag of this and this only: That you understand and know me. I'm GOD, and I act in loyal love. I do what's right and set things right and fair, and delight in those who do the same things. These are my trademarks.*

> —Jeremiah 9:23–24 MSG

GOD's Decree:

> *But let him that glorieth glory in this, that he understandeth and knoweth me, that I am the LORD which exercise lovingkindness, judgment, and righteousness, in the earth: for in these things I delight, saith the LORD.*

> —Jeremiah 9:24 KJV

Benefit/Provision #7—There are legions of angels helping us, for which the world has no counter-measures

> *The angel of the LORD encampeth round about them that fear him, and delivereth them.*

> —Psalm 34:7 KJV

> *The angel of the LORD camps around those who fear God, and he saves them.*

> —Psalm 34:7 NCV

Benefit/Provision #8—Faith sees things that are out of sight

> *Are they not all ministering spirits, sent forth to minister for them who shall be heirs of salvation?*

> —Hebrews 1:14 KJV

> *All angels are spirits who serve. God sends them to serve those who will receive salvation.*

> —Hebrews 1:14 NIRV

Allow God to Use You

There is no past too troubled and no person that God cannot redeem. He took a murderer name Moses and made him a prophet. He took a liar and cheat named Jacob and made him a prince named Israel and blessed his seed. He took a prostitute named Rahab, called her blessed, and changed her profession. He took a Christian hater named Saul and made him a great apostle—Paul.

Skilled workers are always in demand and admired.

"Seeth thou a man diligent in his business? He shall stand before kings; he shall not stand before mean men" (Proverbs 22:29). Every step counts. You are headed in the right direction when you walk with God. It is important to stay spiritually fit by walking with God, which *The Holy Bible* describes as an intimate, growing relationship with the Lord. Enoch walked with God three hundred years (Genesis 5:22). Noah was a just man, perfect in his generations. Noah walked with God (Genesis 6:9). Both men are mentioned in the Book of Hebrews, chapter 11, where they are commended for their faith. Enoch, in verse 5, was translated that he should not see death. Noah, in verse 7, moved with fear and built an ark to the saving of his house. The work Jesus accomplished for us, the Spirit now accomplishes for us. The spirit searches all things. God always communicates with our spirit (emphasis added below).

> *But as it is written, EYE HATH NOT SEEN, NOR EAR HEARD, NEITHER HAVE ENTERED INTO THE HEART OF MAN, THE THINGS WHICH GOD HATH PREPARED FOR THEM THAT LOVE HIM. But God hath revealed then unto us by His Spirit; for the Spirit searcheth all things, yea, the deep things of God.*
>
> —1 Corinthians 2:9–10 KJV

> *That is what the Scriptures mean when they say, No eye has seen, no ear has heard, and no mind has imagined what God has prepared for those who love him."[a]10 But[b] it was to us that God revealed these things by his Spirit. For his Spirit searches out everything and shows us God's deep secrets.*
>
> —1 Corinthians 2:9–10 NLT

Divine Assignment

This touching story reveals the power of God:

For twenty-eight years, God has blessed my husband, Joe, in this military career. We have had our share of roadblocks along the way, all of which have been opportunities for us to remember to focus on the Giver and the gifts.

I remember when my husband was a major, preparing to graduate from the Command and General Staff College in Kansas. He wanted to be assigned as a staff officer in a battalion, in hopes that one day he might qualify for a command. This was a path that career Army officers needed to take, and it was a path that we were prepared for.

"Lord please position me in this type of job. Please guide me with Your hand," Joe prayed throughout his year of school, which finally came to an end. Graduation day was here, and we were going to see what was on the horizon. It was an exciting time. We waited in anticipation for the assignments officer in Washington, DC, to call and tell us the next step of our military journey.

Prior to flying to Germany after accepting an operations officer position, we visited Joe's parents in California, and while there, received a phone call from his branch headquarters that would turn our lives upside down.

"The Chief of Staff of the Army needs a travel officer, Major, and the job is yours if you want it."

"Thanks, let me think about it ..." was all that Joe could reply.

He longed for the opportunity to command a battalion. Left with the decision, we did the only thing we knew to do: Pray.

The next morning, the phone rang again. "Major, we decided to offer the job to another person. If you want the opportunity to command, you need to serve as a staff officer in a battalion now."

My husband eventually did command a battalion, and we have learned through the years, whether in prosperity or testing, to seek God's guidance through prayer. We know that all the details of our lives have been directed, just as God has orchestrated believers from the foundation of the world. In His grace, God provided prayer—a way for us to express our faith in Him, that His presence and love might be a reality in our lives. For He has always known the desires of our hearts.

Source: *God Answers Prayers*, Military Edition: True Stories from People Who Serve and Those Who Love Them, Allison Bottke with Cheryll Hutchings and Jennifer Devlin. Story by Wendy Fil, p. 176.

Gifts

Your gifts and talents do not tell everything about you, they are just expressions of the things that you are able to do. When God made you, He made you to be something more than just the talents you and others see. Your gifts and talents have been carefully designed for you, and they can be only as good as you make them to be. Don't sweat it if people don't think you have skill, just stay focused, embrace your calling, and walk in God's will. Your gift is what God gave you to bring honor to Him, so keep your eyes on the prize and don't worry about other people. As you work every day to develop your gift, God will send you the right people to give you a lift. Whether they do or don't, know that you'll be okay, because the success of your life doesn't depend on them anyway. Remember that it is totally up to you to make it or break it, but remember if you don't use that gift, God just might take it.

All Authority is Ordained of God

Stay under authority. It is God's plan to protect your life. The higher powers are established by God as expressly stated in Titus 3:1, 1 Peter 2:13, and Acts 5:29. As a parent protects their sons and daughters, God protects His children. As a boss protects his/her staff, God protects His children. As pastors protect and pray for their congregations, God protects His children. It is ordained by God that we respect and obey those in leadership. Staying under authority serves as protection, even though we may not "see" its benefits. It is a spiritual law.

> *Everyone must submit to governing authorities. For all authority comes from God, and those in positions of authority have been placed there by God.*
>
> —Romans 13:1 NLT

> *Let every soul be subject unto the higher powers. For there is no power but of God: the powers that be are ordained of God.*
>
> —Romans 13:1 KJV

> *The higher powers are established by God. Respect and obey the authority that has been placed over you, for that is your protection.*
>
> *Put them in mind to be subject to principalities and powers, to obey magistrates, to be ready to every good work.*
>
> —Titus 3:1 KJV

> *Remind them to be subject to rulers and authorities, to obey, to be ready for every good work.*
>
> —Titus 3:1 NKJV

Christian citizenship requires us to be subject to those in positions of authority. Obey their instruction and stay ready to work.

For the Lord's sake, yield to the people who have authority in this world: the king, who is the highest authority, and the leaders who are sent by him to punish those who do wrong and to praise those who do right.

—1 Peter 2:13–14 NCV

Submit yourselves to every ordinance of man for the Lord's sake: whether it be to the king, as supreme; Or unto governors, as unto them that are sent by him for punishment of evildoings, and for the praise of them that do well.

—1 Peter 2:13–14 KJV

Be obedient to natural laws, for the Lord's sake, as well as spiritual laws.

We ought to obey God rather than men.

—Acts 5:29 KJV

We must obey God, not human authority!

—Acts 5:29 NCV

Seek to please and obey our Heavenly Father first and foremost in your life.

NOTES:

_____

_____

_____

_____

Get Prepared

Like it or not, we are all facing a workplace future that will be a close replica of changing jobs and changing careers. Even in the fast and fluid 2011 economy, workers were losing, finding, abandoning, and embracing jobs at fast-forward speed. A recent survey from the U.S. Census Bureau reports that the difference in lifetime earnings between a high school diploma and a bachelor's degree is about one million dollars! Those with professional degrees earn much more—about 4.4 million dollars during their working life. It is never too late to go back to school or to sharpen your skills about the trends in the job market. Many adults, and young people, have revamped their careers mid-stream and earned additional or new degrees. With advances in technology, you can now earn your degree online, from an accredited college or university, in your spare time and from the comfort of your own home. The following are helpful online resources as you carefully plan your career progression:

A Web Tutorial

Most accredited colleges and universities offer online degree programs in a variety of career fields. These institutions of higher learning have websites that list all of their services, including the online course offerings and schedules. To learn more about these courses, visit their advertised websites.

Prepping for a job interview:

- www.hoovers.com—Thousands of company capsules outline financial data, list key competitors, and link to related news articles.
- www.newslink.org—Find out what's being said about a company in its hometown with these links to newspapers across the country. For example, the volume of job openings posted on one company website worried a job seeker. Was the company growing or having trouble retaining staff? A search of the local paper's site turned up articles dishing on the company's reputation as a hard place to work.
- www.work.com—A search turns up company's press releases. Show you've done your homework by referencing their latest marketing information (Sage Dillon).

Show yourself the money:

- www.salary.com—The broadest salary-compensation site. Its Salary Wizard allows you to pick a job category and a region and to quickly find median salaries by position. There's also news on compensation and benefit trends.
- www.wageweb.com—Designed for human-resource professionals who pay $169 to $219 annually for detailed salary data, the site lets others surf salaries on a national basis for free. Information is current, drawn from surveys of its members, making it a good benchmarking tool.
- www.nationjob.com—This database for job seekers allows you to search by salary level.
- www.bls.gov/ocohome.htm—At this Department of Labor site, you can determine which jobs have good growth prospects and median annual salaries.
- www4.webpoint.com/townnews_job/reloc_calc3.htm—Seeking a quieter life but afraid you can't match your existing salary in your hometown? With this calculator, select the city you live in, the city you'd like to move to, and your salary to see how many bucks you'll need for the same bang (Tim Smart).

Other key information:

- Call 1 (800) 526-7234—The Job Accommodation Network advises employers and employees about workplace accommodations
- www.eeoc.gov—Equal Employment Opportunity Commission
- www.usdoj.gov—Department of Justice

Rethinking To-Do Lists

Keeping a to-do list seems to be an almost universal business practice, particularly for managers who juggle multiple tasks. But many experts believe lists can be counterproductive, giving people a false sense of organization without the benefit of any real planning or prioritization. Disadvantages of to-do lists include are that:

- Provide too many options. The human brain can handle about seven choices before it becomes overwhelmed.

- They tend to include a range of tasks of varying complexity. The user is bound to tick off the small projects and let the most challenging one languish.

- They tend to vary in importance, allowing people to take care of top priorities while letting lower priority tasks fall by the wayside until they become top priorities.

- They do not provide context. To decide which task should be tackled, a manager should know the necessary steps for completion and whether or not the required time and resources are available.

- Nothing about a to-do list prevents a manager from choosing a more tolerable task over the most important and often more difficult one.

Source: *Government Executive*: Management Matters, December 5, 2012, by Elizabeth Newell Jochum and *A Factory of One: Applying Lean Principles to Banish Waste and Improve Your Personal Performance* (Productivity Press: December 2011), by Daniel Markovitz.

NOTES:

_____

_____

_____

_____

Questions for Personal Reflection or Group Discussion

1. Which of the eight benefits/provisions apply to you? Why?

   _____

   _____

   _____

2. Staying connected to God during the developmental phases at work is vitally important. Give some examples.

   _____

   _____

   _____

3. Allowing God to use you in the workplace can and will inspire others to excel. Do you believe this? Why?

   _____

   _____

   _____

4. Describe three ways that you prepared for your current position at work.

   _____

   _____

   _____

5. Development and preparation are recurring activities. What steps have you taken recently to develop your skills and talents?

   _____

   _____

   _____

food for thought

ON DEVELOPMENT

Acres of Diamonds — Part I

In 1870, journalist Russell Conwell was traveling in what was then Mesopotamia, when he heard the tale of a prosperous Persian farmer, Ali Hafed. Lured by stories of fabulous hidden wealth, he deserted his fruitful farm in search of a mythical diamond field. Far and wide he roamed, but he never found his dream. Eventually, he died a disillusioned pauper. Not long afterwards, acres of diamonds were found on Ail Hafed's land.

Conwell discovered a great truth in this story: Your diamonds are not in far-away mountains or distant seas; they are in your own backyard if you will dig for them. Although he went on to author 40 books and was a famous orator, Conwell is most remembered for his lecture entitled, "*Acres of Diamonds*," that he delivered more than 6,000 times in towns across America.

Source: Hansen, Mark V. and Robert G. Allen. *The One Minute Millionaire,* Daily Millionaire Minutes ©2002.

Chapter Three

Maturity

"In all human affairs there are things both certain and doubtful, and both are equally in the hands of God, who is accustomed to guide to a good end the causes that are just and are sought with diligence."

—Isabella of Spain, 1451–1504

For not from the east nor from the west nor from the south come promotion and lifting up. *But God is the Judge! He puts down one and lifts up another.*

—Psalm 75:6–7 AMP

For promotion cometh neither from the east, nor from the west, nor from the south. But God is the judge: he putteth down one, and setteth up another.

—Psalm 75:6–7 KJV

Responsibility and accountability are measures of maturity.

*E*xcellence never happens by accident. We have to make it happen. Our methods matter every bit as much as our results. Excellence is a *process*, not just an outcome.

Maturity, then, is a direct result of excellence. How we react to the situations, people, and circumstances on the job is manifested through our maturity. Maturity, as used in *The Holy Bible*, also means "*perfected*." In the Greek—*teleios*—it has two meanings:

(1) "Having reached its end," and

(2) "Finished, complete, perfect."

It is used of persons primarily of physical development, then, with ethical import, "fully grown, mature"—1 Corinthians 2:6; 14:20, Ephesians 4:13, Philippians 3:15, Colossians 1:28, 4:12, Hebrews 5:14—Fully grown or of full age.

> *Howbeit we speak wisdom among them that are perfect: yet not the wisdom of this world, nor of the princes of this world, that come to nought.*
>
> —1 Corinthians 2:6 KJV

> *However, I speak a wisdom to those who are mature. But this wisdom is not from this world or from the rulers of this world, who are losing their power.*
>
> —1 Corinthians 2:6 NCV

Other variations of *maturity* include:

'*Perfect*' refers to the morally and spiritually *mature*—

> *Brothers and sisters, stop thinking like children. Be like babies as far as evil is concerned. But be grown up in your thinking.*
>
> —1 Corinthians 14:20 NIRV

> *Brethren, be not children in understanding: howbeit in malice be ye children, but in understanding be men.*
>
> —1 Corinthians 14:20 KJV

Be *mature* as it relates to understanding—

Greek word	Meaning	Three-fold meaning when used together
Ginoskō	To allow oneself to learn	(1) To allow oneself to increase in knowledge; (2) To learn by use and practice; and
Manthanō	To understand learning	(3) To allow understanding by an act of one's will.

Till we all come in the unity of the faith, and of the knowledge of the Son of God, unto a perfect man, unto the measure of the stature of the fullness of Christ.

—Ephesians 4:13 KJV

Till we all come to the unity of the faith and of the knowledge of the Son of God, to a perfect man, to the measure of the stature of the fullness of Christ;

—Ephesians 4:13 NKJV

Maturity requires us to continually seek after the knowledge of God:

So let's keep focused on that goal, those of us who want everything God has for us. If any of you have something else in mind, something less than total commitment, God will clear your blurred vision—you'll see it yet! Now that we're on the right track, let's stay on it.

—Philippians 3:15–16 MSG

Let us therefore as many as be perfect, be thus minded: and if any thing ye be otherwise minded, God shall reveal even this unto you.

—Philippians 3:15 KJV

Perfect, or mature, requires us to have the mind of Christ and to be serious about the Great Commandment of God—Go ye therefore, and teach all nations, baptizing them in the name of the Father, and of the Son, and of the Holy Ghost: Teaching them to observe all things whatsoever I have commanded you: and, lo, I am with you always, even unto the end of the world (Matthew 28:19–20).

Whom ye preach, warning every man, and teaching every man in all wisdom; that we may present every man perfect in Christ Jesus.

—Colossians 1:28 KJV

We preach about him. With all the wisdom we have, we warn and teach everyone. When we bring them to God, we want them to be perfect as people who belong to Christ.

—Colossians 1:28 NIRV

Consistently and persistently spread the good news of Jesus Christ. Have a desire in your heart to let everyone know that Jesus is Lord.

Epaphras, who is one of you, a servant of Christ, saluteth you, always labouring fervently for you in prayers, that ye may stand perfect and complete in all the will of God.

—Colossians 4:12 KJV

Epaphras, who is one of yourselves, a servant of Christ Jesus, sends you greetings. [He is] always striving for you earnestly in his prayers, [pleading] that you may [as persons of ripe character and clear conviction] stand firm and mature [in spiritual growth], convinced and fully assured in[a]everything willed by God.

—Colossians 4:12 AMP

You may appear perfect and fully assured in all His will. It means literally to the Colossians being ushered into God's heavenly presence in a morally perfect state—

Solid food is for those who are mature, who through training have the skill to recognize the difference between right and wrong.

—Hebrews 5:14 NLT

But strong meat belongeth to them that are of full age, even those who by reason of use have their senses exercised to discern both good and evil.

—Hebrews 5:14 KJV

To be mature means to be complete, finished and grown up in the things of God. No more struggles with the basic principles of Christianity, but having moved on to become mature representatives of Christ in this earth: On our jobs; during our team meetings; before our customers; during strategy sessions; while training others for their jobs; in good times; and during troubled times.

Blessed is the man who finds out which way God is moving and then gets going in the same direction.

NOTES:

_____

_____

_____

_____

CNN Heroes

Since 2007, *Cable News Network* (CNN) hosts an annual awards show to recognize and honor great servants throughout the world based upon their exceptional service to their local communities. In a deliberate move, the shows' producer and director solicit the assistance of celebrities to bestow the honors upon the ten winners (heroes) that includes a $50,000 grant for their work. The CNN Hero of the Year is awarded a grant of $250,000.

In 2012, Thulani Madondo, Director, Kliptown Youth Program, was one of the ten recipients of the annual CNN Heroes Award. Kliptown is 15 miles from the township of Johannesburg, South Africa, in the heart of Soweto, a nearby slum with a population of approximately 40,000. Thulani's personal story is noteworthy and a testament to his resiliency and perseverance. His youth program provides clothes, school uniforms, tutoring, meals, and activities to 400 children in the Kliptown community. He states, "We're trying to give them the sense that everything is possible." Thulani is:

- One of nine children;
- A child raised by his aunt;
- The only one among his siblings not to drop out of school.

Thulani was thirty years old at the time of the CNN awards ceremony. Twenty-one of the children that attended his youth program have gone on to universities.

His full story is posted here: http://www.cnn.com/SPECIALS/cnn.heroes/2012.heroes/thulani.madondo.html.

Ways to Improve Your Public Speaking

As we mature, sharing knowledge through our words will become more important. Toastmasters, the nonprofit dedicated to teaching public speaking and leadership skills, offers ten tips for public speaking, many of which managers can apply to daily interactions with their team. For example, **know your material.** Speak on a topic on which you are well-versed so you can talk knowledgeably without memorization.

Practice, practice, practice. Doing this before a major speech is a no-brainer. But managers should practice for smaller interactions too. Toastmasters advises public speakers **not to apologize** for any nervousness or any hiccups that occur during delivery. After all, audiences likely will not notice small slip-ups.

Finally, **realize that people want you to succeed.** Just as audiences root for the speaker addressing them, genuinely wanting them to be interesting, stimulating, informative, and entertaining, managers' subordinates know that their work experiences will be exponentially better if their boss is successful.

Source: *Government Executive,* "Management Matters," by Elizabeth Newell Jochum, November 21, 2012.

Change Will Cause Maturity

Change is life giving. It helps us grow into someone greater than we already are. If you're not riding the wave of change, you'll find yourself beneath it. Sometimes in the waves of change, we find our true direction.

In this rapidly changing society, we find ourselves in a constant state of transition. What currently works becomes outdated in a hurry. Three key factors drive change in life and in the workplace:

- People
- Technology
- Information

People create change. Scientific evidence reveals that human creation is six or seven million years old. It took that long for the population of the earth to reach 5.3 billion people. Predictions say it will take only about fifty years for the next 5.3 billion people to inhabit the earth. If people create change—and we do—then we should expect a rapid increase in the rate of change as the population doubles in the next few decades.

Technology, too, creates change. Evidence will prove that approximately eighty percent of our technological inventions have occurred since 1900. It was predicted that within the last fifteen years of the twentieth century, we would see as much technological change as there was in the first eighty-five years. It is literally multiplying on a daily basis.

Information and *knowledge* is power! There was more information produced in the thirty years between 1965 and 1995 than was produced in the entire 5,000-year period from 3000 B.C. to 1965. Information available in the world is doubling every five years and is becoming available to many more people than it ever reached before. Far more knowledge, reaching far more people, far faster than ever before. A better informed population means better chances for change.

Change has no conscience. It does not play favorites and takes no prisoners. Unfortunately, it does ruthlessly destroy organizations with cultures that do not adapt. Observe what has happened to multiple companies over the past five years and the devastating impact on their employees. A world of high-velocity change calls for radical shifts in behavior and a reliance upon the One who does not change—God Almighty.

NOTES:

_____

_____

_____

_____

Maturity in the Workplace

A View of the Federal Government Workplace

Our goal is to make the entire federal government both less expensive and more efficient, and to change the culture of our national bureaucracy away from complacency and entitlement toward initiative and empowerment. We intend to redesign, to reinvent, and reinvigorate the entire national government.

> —President Bill Clinton
> Remarks announcing the National Performance Review,
> March 3, 1993

In 1993, the Clinton Administration took on a bold and daunting task—to reform the Federal Government. It was called *The National Performance Review*. It is about change—*historic change*—in the way the government works. Its four-fold mission was as follows:

- Cutting red tape (the bureaucracy),

- Putting customers first (service is key),

- Empowering employees to get results (valuing human resources for the asset that they are), and

- Cutting back to basics (taking common sense to higher places).

I am proud to have participated in this dynamic project for six years, from 1993 to 1999, specifically in the area of procurement reform. Assignments at the Office of Federal Procurement Policy (OFPP) in Washington, DC, being called by the Administrator of OFPP to give testimony before the United States House of Representatives Committee on Small Business, and presentations before the National Contract Management World Congress, on three occasions, were hallmark events during my twenty-seven-year government career.

The core of The National Performance Review is expressly articulated in unison by President Clinton and Vice President Gore:

We can no longer afford to pay more for—and get less from—our government. The answer for every problem cannot always be another program or more money. It is time to radically change the way government operates—to shift from top-down bureaucracy to entrepreneurial government that empowers citizens and communities to change our country from the bottom up. We must reward the people and ideas that work and get rid of those that don't.

Reduce paperwork?

A government that works better and costs less requires efficient and effective information systems. The Paperwork Reduction Act of 1995 and the Information Technology Management Reform Act of 1996 provide the opportunity to improve significantly the way the Federal Government acquires and manages information technology. Agencies now have the clear authority and responsibility to make measurable improvements in mission performance and service delivery to the public through the strategic application of information technology. A coordinated approach that builds on existing structures and successful practices is needed to provide maximum benefit across the Federal Government from this technology. Accordingly, by the authority vested in me as President by the Constitution and the laws of the United States of America, it is hereby ordered as follows ...

—Opening paragraphs of ***Executive Order 13011***, Federal Information Technology, July 16, 1996, William Jefferson Clinton, President of the United States.

The eleven sections in this Executive Order define the policies and procedures that will govern the strategic shift of the Federal Government into the information age. Section One states, in part, that the policy of the United States Government is that executive agencies shall:

(a) Significantly improve the management of their information systems, including the acquisition of information technology;

(b) Refocus information technology management to support directly their strategic missions;

(c) Establish clear accountability for information resources management activities by creating agency Chief Information Officers (CIO's) with the visibility and management responsibilities necessary to advise the agency head on the design, development, and implementation of those information systems;

(d) Cooperate in the use of information technology to improve the productivity of federal programs and to promote a coordinated, interoperable, secure, and shared government-wide infrastructure that is provided and supported by a diversity of private sector suppliers and a well-trained corps of information technology professionals;

(e) Establish an interagency support structure that builds on existing successful interagency efforts.

Employee's Views

Adherence to the Merit Principles in the Workplace, Federal Employee's Views, is a Federal Government study of the workplace environment. This report was compiled and issued by the U.S. Merit Systems Protection Board, Office of Policy and Evaluation, as a report to the President and Congress of the United States. The report summarized the responses from 9,710 federal employees, in 1997, who were asked to assess the extent to which their respective agencies take actions that are consistent with the merit principles. Its goal is to obtain the views of federal employees on a number of workplace issues such as working conditions, job satisfaction, and the quality of coworkers and supervisors. The merit system principles embody a set of values that lie at the heart of public service, and their purpose is to ensure that the trust that the public has placed in the Federal Government to operate a personnel system based on merit is earned.

The Merit System Principles, which were articulated in statute in the 1978 Civil Service Reform Act, are a set of values for federal public service that date back to the beginning of the merit-based civil service system in 1883. The principles address basic human resource management activities. These activities—including selections, promotions, and actions to deal with performance problems—define the goals that all federal managers are expected to strive for when managing their workforce. They are meant to ensure that processes and systems the government uses for selecting and maintaining the federal workforce will result in a competent workforce that serves the best interests of the American people. These questions were asked of employees of every grade plus the Senior Executive Service as part of the 1996 Merit Principles Survey, a government-wide survey that MSPB has conducted approximately every three years since 1983 to assess the health of the merit system. These results are from the twentieth anniversary of the 1978 Civil Service Reform Act was approaching. Substantial minorities of respondents believed violations were occurring that undermine the merit system. The findings of this fifth survey, since 1983, are mixed:

- According to employees, budget cuts, downsizing, and reinvention efforts have had noticeable effects, both positive and negative, on the operation of many federal organizations.
- Efforts to reinvent the way the government does business have not been pursued to the same degree by all agencies.
- Results of reinvention efforts are mixed overall.
- Employees have a positive view of their jobs and organizations.
- Problem employees remain a significant problem for many federal supervisors.
- Employees continue to be concerned about prohibited personnel practices.

Based upon the key findings and results of the 1996 Merit Principles Survey, the following recommendations were made:

- Agencies and organizations should make sure that their efforts to reduce expenditures also include a sincere effort to involve employees in attempts to improve their operations.
- In many federal organizations there is a culture that sanctions not dealing effectively with problem employees. This must be changed for the government to be able to hold employees accountable for their performance.
- Efforts should be made by the Office of Personnel Management and individual agencies to ensure that the government maintains its ability to find and recruit high-quality applicants.
- In a time of greater decentralization and delegation of personnel management authorities, it is increasingly important to ensure that there is an effective and visible system in place to ensure that supervisors are held accountable for the decisions they make.

A View of the Corporate Workplace

*The quest for excellence into the twentieth-first century begins in the schoolroom, but we must go next to the **workplace**. More than 20 million new jobs will be created before the new century unfolds and by then our economy should be able to provide a job for everyone who wants to work. We must enable our workers to adapt to the rapidly changing nature of the workplace ...*

—President Ronald Reagan
State of the Union Address
January 27, 1987

In an executive summary prepared by the Hudson Institute of Indianapolis, Indiana entitled, *"Workforce 2000—Work and Workers for the 21st Century,"* June 1987, it was predicted that four trends would shape the last years of the twentieth century:

1. The American economy should grow at relatively healthy pace
2. Despite its international comeback, U.S. manufacturing will be a much smaller share of the economy in the year 2000.
3. The workforce will grow slowly, becoming older, more female, and more disadvantaged. Only fifteen percent of the new entrants to the labor force over the next thirteen years will be native white males, compared to forty-seven percent in that category in 1987.
4. The new jobs in service industries will demand much higher skill levels than the jobs in the middle 1980s.

The executive summary left us with six challenges:

1. Stimulating Balanced World Growth
2. Accelerating Productivity Increases in Service Industries
3. Maintaining the Dynamism of an Aging Workforce
4. Reconciling the Conflicting Needs of Women, Work, and Families
5. Integrating Black and Hispanic Workers Fully into the Economy.

Unfortunately, instead of responding to President Reagan's challenge to enable our workers to adapt to the rapidly changing nature of the workplace, the corporate workplace has become mired in its own love for money, greed, speed to market, and latest management fads that have failed its citizens. Conversely, the six challenges from the Hudson Institute's *Workforce 2000* prediction have only gained minimal momentum as the day-to-day focus on profits and speed deflect the good intentions of the report.

In June 2002, President George W. Bush outlined a ten-point plan that will improve corporate responsibility and help protect America's shareholders. These proposals are guided by the following core principles:

1. Providing better information to investors;
2. Making corporate officers more accountable; and
3. Developing a stronger, more independent audit system.

Proposals one and two come under the subheading—**Better Information for Investors**. Proposals three through six come under the subheading—**Making Corporate Officers Accountable**.

Proposals seven through ten come under the subheading—**Developing a Strong, More Independent Audit System**. In an excerpt from a June 28, 2002 speech on corporate responsibility, Mr. Bush says, "We expect high standards in our schools; we expect high standards in corporate offices as well. And I intend to enforce the law to make sure that there are high standards." (For more information on the President's Ten-Point Plan, see http://www.whitehouse.gov.news/releases/2002/03/20020307.html)

Understanding Diversity

Cultural diversity is an essential part of the workplace that had gained momentum between 1996 to 2008. Countless numbers of dollars, energy, and resources have been expended on attempts—some successful, some wasteful—to "level the playing field" and promote "fair access" to all who desire an equal opportunity to compete for jobs. In article entitled, *"Has 'Minority' Become a Dirty Word?,"* by Yoji Cole, the author best summarizes why man's solution to a God-ordained calling will not and cannot work for the benefit of all that are involved:

> *The politically correct speakers in the nation have gone from using "Negro" to "black" to "African American;" from using "Spanish" to "Hispanic" to "Latino;" from using "Oriental" to "Asian" to "Asian American." Then, of course, there is the all-encompassing word "minority." "Minority," however, is falling out of favor with a growing number of people throughout the country. People who would rather see the word disappear from colonial English dictionary say the word has become a stamp for those who lack proper education, economic opportunity that lacked drive, initiative, and a pursuit of excellence. In effect, "minority," has become the stereotype. "When people are afraid to speak about issues of race because they might use the wrong word and then get slammed, they stop talking," says Howard Ross, President of diversity consultants Cook Ross, Inc. "The most important thing that people can, and should do, if we are going to move forward regarding these issues, is to be talking."*
>
> <u>Source</u>: *Diversity Inc.com*, February 11, 2002.

Today's workforce includes more women—increasingly in high paying professions such as law—but far fewer seniors and farmers.

A View of the Workplace in General Terms & Growth over a Decade

Working Category	1900	2000
Married Women in Labor Force	8%	61% (1998)
Single Women in Labor Force	44%	69% (1998)
Men Over 65 in Labor Force	63%	17% (1998)
Female Lawyers	1%	29% (1998)
Factory Workers' Hourly Wage *(inflation adjusted)*	$3.80 (1909)	$13.90 (1999)
Union Members *(share of civilian labor force)*	3%	12% (1998)
Family Farms	5.7 million	1.9 million (1997)
War Veterans	1.1 million	25.1 million (1998)

Source: *U.S. News and World Report*, Cover Story—"Who We Were, Who We are America 1900–2000 How an Epic Century Changed a Nation," August 6, 2001, page 18, and "The First Measured Century," U.S. Census Bureau, Statistical Abstract of the United States.

NOTES:

_____

_____

_____

_____

Promotion Comes from God

For promotion cometh neither from the east, nor from the west, nor from the south. But God is the judge: he putteth down one, and setteth up another.

—Psalm 75:6–7 KJV

The wise are neither young nor old—their physical age tells us nothing, and more than the generality of men can be divided between age and youth on the basis of their knowledge. The wise are always young in will and energy and old in experience and reflection.

—Frances Lischner

Daniel

Daniel was a governmental officer and prophet of God (Daniel 1:1–6 and Matthew 24:15). As a young Jew he was taken captive and trained for service in the Babylonian royal court. He served in influential positions under four kings—Nebuchadnezzar, Belshazzar, Darius, and Cyrus. He firmly refused to do anything contrary to God's teachings, even when it meant risking his life (Daniel 1:8 and 6:7–16). Daniel's gift of prophecy was evidenced early in life as his name means *God is my judge*.

The Old Testament Book of Daniel depicts Daniel's loyalty to God in the face of imprisonment, pagan religion, and false teaching. It also includes Daniel's visions. He was frequently pushed to compromise his faith, but he did not. His well-known choices include insisting on eating a healthy diet (chapter 1), worshiping God rather than avoiding the fiery furnace (chapter 3), interpreting the writing on the wall (chapter 5), and praying to God rather than avoiding the lion's den (chapter 6).

The last portion of the book—chapters 7 through 12—records visions God gave to Daniel that depicts Israel's future. This portion of Daniel is apocalyptic literature; it tells about the future with symbols and signs. These passages give hope that the cruelty will end and God's triumph will become obvious. Because Daniel showed his faith, Kings Nebuchadnezzar and Darius honored God.

Titus

Titus was a Greek Christian coworker with the Apostle Paul. Paul may have converted Titus to Christ (Titus 1:4). He traveled on missionary journeys with Paul and took Paul's first letter to the Corinthians with the assignment of helping the church correct its problems (2 Corinthians 7:13–15).

The New Testament Book of Titus is a book of encouragement in the face of opposition, from Paul to Titus. Paul reminds Titus to hold onto sound faith and sound doctrine, to urge him to seek Christian leaders with good character, and to show him how to teach.

Timothy

Timothy was a native of Lystra who learned the scriptures from his Jewish mother Eunice and grandmother Lois (Acts 16:1 and 2 Timothy 1:5). His father was a Greek. Timothy means *honoring God*, and that he did as he served alongside the Apostle Paul, who was his father in the faith (1 Timothy 1:2). Timothy accompanied Paul on missionary journeys and was listed along with Paul in the sending of six letters:

- Second Corinthians
- Philippians
- Colossians
- First and Second Thessalonians
- Philemon

The New Testament Books of Timothy were books Paul wrote to a young Christian co-worker named Timothy. First Timothy warns against false teaching. It also gives instructions for church worship, presents characteristics of church leaders, and encourages Christian service. Second Timothy, written near the end of Paul's life, gives encouraging advice to Timothy including how to endure and to serve Christ faithfully.

Take Heed to Wise Counsel

We gain insight when we listen to those who have gone before and know more than we do—insight we miss when our pride stands in the way. We are able to learn from others when we humble ourselves and acknowledge how little we really know. Willingness to learn is a mark of those who are truly wise.

Consider our Lord as a boy, "sitting in the midst of teachers, both listening to them and asking them questions" (Luke 2:46). Proverbs 1:5 says that "*a wise man will hear and increase learning, and a man of understanding will attain wise counsel.*" If you think you know everything, you have a lot to learn. Even Jesus increased in wisdom.

And Jesus increased in wisdom and stature, and in favor with God and man.

—Luke 2:52 KJV

Jesus grew in wisdom and in stature and in favor with God and all the people.

—Luke 2:52 NLT

NOTES:

_____

_____

_____

_____

Be Prepared for Job Uncertainty

Reinventing yourself professionally does not necessarily mean changing jobs. You can make strategic moves without leaving your job. While on the job, ask yourself what you want to do in your current job. Go ahead and explore the following options:

- - Join professional organizations in your industry
- - Enlist a career coach or counselor to help you with your career move
- - Volunteer to serve on outside organizations, especially when it improves skills that will be noticeable back on the job.

<u>Source</u>: Genovese, Peter, "Taking the Plunge, Ditching Corporate Life? Think Swan Dive, Not Belly-Flop," *The Sunday Star Ledger Newspaper*, October 20, 2002.

Ten tips for job seekers:

1. **Gauge your finances** and build reserves to survive six months of unemployment.
2. **Don't take the first job** that comes your way out of desperation. Consider taking a temporary job to get through the financial times.
3. **Sign up for unemployment** right away.
4. **Take advantage of COBRA** health insurance coverage.
5. **Keep your skills up to date.** There are government-funded nonprofit agencies that offer free retraining.
6. **Don't get down on yourself.** There's a mourning period after a layoff, which most people don't expect. But remember, layoffs are not the fault of the workers. After the massive growth of the late nineties, layoffs were inevitable. If you can afford it, take a brief vacation.
7. **Keep yourself on a schedule.** Set your alarm clock, go to the gym, surf the Web for job listings, work on your resume, and meet friends for coffee. If you have a routine, that's going to spur your momentum.
8. **Separate your past from your future.** If you go into an interview feeling angry about your last situation, that will come through in the interview. If need be, take an hour before meeting with a potential employer to think about how you can add value to that company.

9. **Take advantage of outplacement** services offered by your former employer. They're free services that can be very valuable. You need to get yourself ready to be competitive. You're entering boot camp.

10. **Don't spam potential employers.** Sending out 700 resumes and form letters is not the way to go. Personalize your resume and cover letters to highlight the strengths each employer is looking for.

<u>Source:</u> Hemming, Allison, "Layoff Lessons Learned," *Computer World News,* February 19, 2002.

A Bevy of Questions from Your Road to Purpose Journey (Malone, 2011):

1. **What did you learn?** This is where you speak to the educational values you gained from your journey.

2. **What did you lose?** This is where you examine the exit of negatives that you possessed when you started this journey but that you now live without because they do not fit into the process of your future life pursuit.

3. **What did you leave?** These are the excessive things that may not have been a negative influence but were an unnecessary attraction or affiliation for where you were headed.

4. **What do you still find lacking?** This is where you expose your vulnerabilities to yourself. Remember, no life study or life journey is a perfect one—especially the first time around.

5. **What do you now long for?** This is where your expectations portray their increase in value and worth. Your present and future outlook should reflect an inconsistency with your past expectations now that you have experienced *The Road to Purpose* challenge.

6. **What does your life speak about you now as a person?** This is where your experiences are expressed concerning the person you were and the person you are now. Write about the new you even if only a few minor character changes are visible.

Anonymity Breeds Contentment

Be content with yourself and the person that God created. Do not seek fame from men. Reflect on the significant actions of these unnamed Biblical characters below and what it means to your salvation experience.

It is better to be faithful than famous

David's soldiers found a young man who had been left behind by a retreating enemy army. The Egyptian slave is not named, but he provided key information that helped David to rescue his family.

And David said unto him, To whom belongest thou? And whence art thou? And he said, I am a young man of Egypt, servant to an Amalekite; and my master left me, because three days agone I fell sick.

—1 Samuel 30:13 KJV

And David said to him, To whom do you belong? And from where have you come? He said, I am a young man of Egypt, servant to an Amalekite; and my master left me because three days ago I fell sick.

—1 Samuel 30:13 AMP

The young boy whose lunch of bread and fish was multiplied by Jesus to feed the thousands:

He said, "Here is a boy with five small loaves of barley bread. He also has two small fish. But how far will that go in such a large crowd?"

—John 6:9 NIRV

There is a lad here, which hath five barley loaves, and two small fishes: but what are they among so many?

—John 6:9 KJV

The owner of the colt on which Jesus rode into Jerusalem:

And sure enough, as they were untying it, the owners asked them, "Why are you untying that colt?"

—Luke 19:33 NLT

And as they were loosing the colt, the owners thereof said unto them, Why loose ye the colt?

—Luke 19:33 KJV

The owner of the house in which Jesus and His disciples ate the Passover:

And ye shall say unto the Goodman of the house, The Master saith unto thee, Where is the guest chamber, where I shall eat the passover with my disciples?

—Luke 22:11 KJV

He said, "Keep your eyes open as you enter the city. A man carrying a water jug will meet you. Follow him home. Then speak with the owner of the house: The Teacher wants to know, 'Where is the guest room where I can eat the Passover meal with my disciples?' He will show you a spacious second-story room, swept and ready. Prepare the meal there."

—Luke 22:10–12 MSG

The boy who saved Paul's life:

But Paul's nephew heard about this plan. So he went into the fort and told Paul.

Then Paul called one of the commanders. He said to him, "Take this young man to the commanding officer. He has something to tell him. So the commander took Paul's nephew to the officer. The commander said, "Paul, the prisoner, sent for me. He asked me to bring this young man to you. The young man has something to tell you. The commanding officer took the young man by the hand. He spoke to him in private. "What do you want to tell me?" the officer asked.

He said, "The Jews have agreed to ask you to bring Paul to the Sanhedrin tomorrow. They will pretend they want more facts about him. ²¹ Don't give in to them. More than 40 of them are waiting in hiding to attack him. They have taken an oath that they will not eat or drink anything until they have killed him. They are ready now. All they need is for you to bring Paul to the Sanhedrin.² The commanding officer let the young man go. But he gave him a warning. "Don't tell anyone you have reported this to me," he said.

—Acts 23:16–22 NIRV

And when Paul's sister's son heard of their lying in wait, he went and entered into the castle, and told Paul. Then Paul called one of the centurions unto him, and said, Bring this young man unto the chief captain: for he hath a certain thing to tell him. So he took him, and brought him to the chief captain, and said, Paul the prisoner called me unto him, and prayed me to bring this young man unto thee, who hath something to say unto thee. Then the chief captain took him by the hand, and went with him aside privately, and asked him, What is that thou hast to tell me?

And he said, The Jews have agreed to desire thee that thou wouldest bring down Paul to morrow into the council, as though they would enquire somewhat of him more perfectly. But do not thou yield unto them: for there lie in wait for him of them more than forty man, which have bound themselves with an oath, that they will neither eat nor drink till looking for a promise from thee. So the chief captain then let the young man depart, and charged him, See thou tell no man that thou hast shewed these things to me.

—Acts 23:16–22 KJV

An anonymous responsibility of anyone in the workplace, or church, is the role of an Armor bearer. The main function of one who is designated as an armor bearer is that of service; he is to help and assist another. Let's look at some of the different forms this service takes.

To this end, an armor bearer …

- Must provide strength for his leader. Always display and produce an attitude of faith and peace.
- Must have a deep-down sense of respect for his leader, and acceptance for, and tolerance of, his leader's personality and his way of doing things.
- Must distinctively understand his leader's thoughts.

- Must walk in agreement with and submission to his leader. In order to be an armor bearer, you must have it settled in your heart that according to Romans 13:1–2, all authority is ordained of God.

- Must make the advancement of his leader his most important goal.

- Must possess endless strength so as to thrust, press, and force his way onward without giving way under harsh treatment.

- Must follow orders immediately and correctly. In order to be a good leader, one must be a good follower.

- Must be a support to his leader.

- Must be an excellent communicator.

- Must have a disposition that will eagerly gain victories for his leader.

- Must have the ability to minister strength and courage to his leader.

Source: Nance, Terry. God's ArmorBearer: How to Serve God's Leaders, 1990.

NOTES:

_____

_____

_____

_____

Questions for Personal Reflection or Group Discussion

1. How do you measure *your* maturity? How about the maturity *of others*?

_____

_____

_____

2. What differentiates a mature versus immature person? Why?

_____

_____

_____

3. While at work, does the maturity of your boss make a huge impact on others? Why or why not?

_____

_____

_____

4. Jesus chose to remain anonymous during His ministry. Why do you think that He chose that option, after all He was the Son of God?

_____

_____

_____

5. During your formative years, your maturity is a catalyst for future success. What Biblical character exemplifies this attribute?

_____

_____

_____

food for thought

ON MATURITY

Remember:

We judge ourselves by our beliefs and intentions, but others judge us by our behaviors and actions.

Police Officer

Construction Worker

Bus Driver

Computer Technician

Entrepreneur

Author

Nurse

Chemist

Sociologist

College Admissions Officer

PART TWO

The Journeyman Years ...
From learning to leading

After the death of Moses the servant of the LORD, *the* LORD *said to Joshua son of Nun, Moses' aide: ² "Moses my servant is dead. Now then, you and all these people, get ready to cross the Jordan River into the land I am about to give to them—to the Israelites. ³ I will give you every place where you set your foot, as I promised Moses. ⁴ Your territory will extend from the desert to Lebanon, and from the great river, the Euphrates—all the Hittite country—to the Mediterranean Sea in the west. ⁵ No one will be able to stand against you all the days of your life. As I was with Moses, so I will be with you; I will never leave you nor forsake you. ⁶ Be strong and courageous, because you will lead these people to inherit the land I swore to their ancestors to give them.⁷ "Be strong and very courageous. Be careful to obey all the law my servant Moses gave you; do not turn from it to the right or to the left, that you may be successful wherever you go.*

—Joshua 1:1–7 NIV

Now after the death of Moses the servant of the LORD it came to pass, that the LORD spake unto Joshua the son of Nun, Moses' minister, saying, Moses my servant is dead; now therefore arise, go over this Jordan, thou, and all this people, unto the land which I do give to them, even to the children of Israel. Every place that the sole of your foot shall tread upon, that have I given unto you, as I said unto Moses ... There shall not any man be able to stand before thee all the days of thy life; as I was with Moses, so I will be with thee: I will not fail thee, nor forsake thee. Be strong and of a good courage: for unto this people shalt thou divide for an inheritance the land, which I sware unto their fathers to give them. Only be thou strong and very courageous, that thou mayest observe to do according to all the law, which Moses my servant commanded thee: turn not from it to the right hand or to the left, that thou mayest prosper whithersoever thou goest.

—Joshua 1:1–3; 5–7 KJV

*T*ransition from a state of learning to leading can be the most challenging—and most rewarding—aspect of one's career. This state requires a different set of challenges, rules, policies, expectations, and values. Preoccupation with *self* must be substituted with a desire to make a positive and constructive impact on your surrounding—*others*. This means to help others achieve their goals while continually striving to improve the workplace for the benefit of everyone.

Joshua was handpicked by God as Moses' successor (Numbers 27) to lead the people of Israel into the promised land—Canaan. God Himself encouraged Joshua because he did not feel that he could handle this awesome task. Through three major military campaigns involving more than thirty enemy armies, the people of Israel learn a crucial lesson under Joshua's leadership. Victory comes through faith in God and obedience to His Word rather than through military might or numerical superiority. His comforting words in chapter one of the Book of Joshua, " ... *be strong and of good courage ...*" (verse 6), are very appropriate during this transitional stage in the life of the worker.

In order to effectively apply what has been learned at the entry level, be guided at all times by God's word—*"Thy word is a lamp unto my feet, and a light onto my path"* (Psalm 119:105). God encourages us to *"acknowledge Him in all thy ways, and He shall direct thy paths"* (Proverbs 3:6). "Paths" is plural, and indicative of all of the options that we will have throughout our working life. Options create choices. Knowing that we will be faced with many, many options, we must not lean on our own understanding, but trust in the Lord with all of your heart (Proverbs 3:5). God is not in the business of disappointing His chosen children!

Having trusted fully in God, the Apostle Paul teaches us to extend kindness and courtesy to everyone, especially to our brothers and sisters in Christ. Our *light*—lifestyle—could be the magnet that eventually draws others to Christ. We are the substance of things hoped for and the evidence that proclaims that God is real although He cannot be seen with the naked eye. *"Be kindly affectioned one to another with brotherly love; in honour preferring one another; Not slothful in business; fervent in spirit; serving the Lord; Rejoicing in hope; patient in tribulation; continuing in prayer"* (Romans 12:10–12). Love never fails because God is love (1 John 4:8).

Lastly, as we transition from learning to leading, we must be watchful as God's chosen overseers on the job. In our new and expanded role, we are responsible to be on alert and watch for situations and circumstances that we can change. *"Ye are all children of light, and the children of the day: we are not of the night, nor of darkness. Therefore let us not sleep, as do others; but let us watch and be sober"* (1 Thessalonians 5:5–6). Be prayerful and vigilant. Show compassion, care, and understanding. Mediate where needed. Solve problems and make decisions based upon God's Word. Demonstrate the peace that passes all understanding while in the midst of tests, temptations, and trials. Dare to launch out into the deep (Luke 5:4)!

Leadership is never about one thing.

Chapter Four

Applying What You Now Know

"We are going to relentlessly chase perfection, knowing full well we will not catch it, because nothing is perfect. But we are going to relentlessly chase it, because in the process we will catch excellence."

—*Vince Lombardi*, former Head Football Coach, Green Bay Packers

*Thy word is a lamp unto my feet, and a **light** onto my path.*

—Psalm 119:105 KJV

Your word is a lamp to guide my feet and a light for my path.

—Psalm 119:105 NLT

Put into practice what you have learned.

*I*n the Book of Joshua, chapter one, the story of the transition in leadership from Moses to Joshua unfolds. Moses had been chosen by God to lead the children of Israel out of the wilderness and into the land that flowed with milk and honey. Through trials and errors, the children of Israel took forty years to travel a distance that should have taken only eleven days. The next generation is led by Moses' successor, Joshua, whose name means "The Lord is Salvation." In the original Greek translation, his name takes on the form *Iēsous,* the same name borne by our Lord, Jesus. The final account of Joshua succeeding Moses is referenced in the book of Deuteronomy, chapter 34. Verse 10 confirms Joshua's Godly appointment inasmuch as stating, *"And there arose not a prophet since in Israel like unto Moses, whom the LORD knew face to face."* This book of Joshua records events that span some forty years. It is considered the first of the Historical Books of the English Bible, because it traces the record of the children of Israel from the shores of the Jordan River to the conquest and division of the land of Canaan. Chapter one begins, *"Now after the death of Moses the servant of the LORD it came to pass, that the LORD spake unto Joshua the son of Nun, Moses' minister, saying ..."* Joshua was Moses' assistant and servant (Exodus 24:13) and successor (Numbers 27:15–23). He served as a military field commander (Exodus 17:9–13), was a spiritual disciple of Moses when he accompanied him up the mountain to receive the Torah (Exodus 24:13), and acted as a believing, courageous spy along with Caleb (Numbers 14:6–10, 30). As Israel's new leader after Moses, he functioned as a military commander taking the land of Canaan and as an administrator in allotting the land. He was a role model for all of Israel's future kings. He was a leader possessing the Lord's spirit and having prophetic sanction (Numbers 27:18 and 22). He was both a military genius and a spiritual giant. He stirred up the faith of his army by ceremony (4:1–7), word (10:25), and life (24:15). He demanded of them exact obedience to the Lord's Word (Joshua 8:35 and 23:6). He lived to be 110 years of age. Furthermore, his acts are noteworthy in the New Testament book of Acts, 7:45. His excellent example of work in the ministry is an inspiration today to all who study this man and how his steps were continually directed by the Lord.

In your heart you plan your life. But the Lord decides where your steps will take you.

—Proverbs 16:9 NIRV

A man's heart deviseth his way: but the LORD directeth his steps.

—Proverbs 16:9 KJV

During this phase in our respective careers, we apply what we now know through the following strategies and attention to detail.

The LORD is sovereign over man's scheming and planning.

Go to now, ye that say, To day or to morrow we will go into such a city, and continue there a year, and buy and sell, and get gain: Whereas ye know not what shall be on the morrow. For what is your life? It is even a vapour, that appeareth for a little time, and then vanisheth away. For that ye ought to say, If the Lord will, we shall live, and do this, or that. But now ye rejoice in your boastings: all such rejoicing is evil. Therefore to him that knoweth to do good, and doeth it not, to him it is sin.

—James 4:13–17 KJV

Come now, you who say, Today or tomorrow we will go into such and such a city and spend a year there and carry on our business and make money. Yet you do not know [the least thing] about what may happen tomorrow. What is the nature of your life? You are [really] but a wisp of vapor (a puff of smoke, a mist) that is visible for a little while and then disappears [into thin air].

You ought instead to say, If the Lord is willing, we shall live and we shall do this or that [thing]. But as it is, you boast [falsely] in your presumption and your self-conceit. All such boasting is wrong. So any person who knows what is right to do but does not do it, to him it is sin.

—James 4:13–17 AMP

Do not pretend, or think, to know something that you do not.

Do not presume to have the resources that you do not. God does have something for Christians to do and we should plan accordingly. We must include God in our plans. Omitting Him is not merely bad planning, it is sin.

It is God's will, not our efforts. Although we need to plan and live responsibly, we are wise to recognize God's control. He is:

- All-powerful (*omnipotent*),
- Occupies all space (*omnipresent*), and
- Infinite in knowledge (*omniscient*). Our unknown future is safe in the hands of the all-knowing God.

Like Joshua, the military man, if we are going to avoid giving too much or too little attention to our work, we need to recognize the other elements of life that deserve our time. In the book, *Your Work Matters to God*, Doug Sherman and William Hendricks mention five parts of life that need our attention. They use the analogy of the sporting event called the pentathlon. In order for an athlete to do well, he must excel in running, swimming, horseback riding, pistol shooting, and fencing. The competitor cannot do well if he focuses on one event at the expense of others, or if he ignores any event. In a similar way, we must devote effort to five basic areas of life if we are to succeed in living as God desires. The five areas are:

Our personal life
Our family
Our church life
Our work
Our community life

NOTES:

_____

_____

_____

_____

Ready for the Transition? Don't Worry

Why do we work? Some do it for love. Others do it for money. But most do it because we have no other choice. Today, our society is dominated by work not seen since the Industrial Revolution. Technology has offered increasing productivity and a higher standard of living for many. Conversely, bank tellers and typists have been replaced by machinery. Employment surveys of today's workers show a decline in job satisfaction. The biggest is workload and workers feel crushed. The advent of technology, ringing cell phones, faxes, and ever-present e-mail have blurred the lines between home and work. Our jobs penetrate every aspect of life. Technology has given us more freedom but has also caused work to occupy us around the clock. "The work ethic and identifying ourselves with work and through work is not alive and well but more present now than at any time in history," says Rutgers University historian John Gillis.

It is beginning to take a toll. One-third of American workers—who work longer hours than their counterparts in any industrialized country—feel overwhelmed by the amount of work they have to do, according to the 2001 Families and Work Institute. In fact, of those surveyed, both men and women wish they were working about eleven hours less per week. However, they do not act upon it as they do not want to be perceived as "less committed." Even the results from the 1973 report entitled, *"Work in America,"* by the Department of Health, Education, and Welfare showed a significant number of Americans were dissatisfied with the quality of their working lives. After decades of abundance, they still did not experience job satisfaction. Dull, repetitive, seemingly meaningless tasks, offering little challenge or autonomy, were causing discontent among workers at all occupational levels. Always a source of pride, the idea that hard work was a calling from God dated to the Reformation and the teachings of Martin Luther. While work had once been a means to serve God, two centuries of choices and industrialization had turned work into an end in itself, stripped of the spiritual meaning that sustained the Puritans who came ready to tame the wilderness.[5]

Consider this:

- U.S. employers reportedly spend $150 to $200 billion annually on stress.
- Forty-four percent of office workers say stress on the job has worsened over the past two years.
- Fifty-two percent of Americans say work is the main cause of stress in their lives.

---

[5] *U.S. News and World Report,* February 2003.

- One out of five workers worldwide admits taking time off from work due to stress.

<u>Source:</u> Pritchett, Price and Ron Pound, *A Survival Guide to the Stress of Organizational Change*, 1995.

Mathematically speaking, it doesn't make sense to worry. Psychologists tell us that roughly 30% of what we worry about never happens; another 30% has already happened; 12% is about unfounded health concerns, and another 20% is about sweating the small stuff. That leaves only 8%. Ninety-two percent of the time we worry for no good reason at all. There is a growing mountain of evidence to suggest that worry is the chief contributor to depression, nervous breakdowns, high blood pressure, heart attacks, and early death. Stress kills. I have never known a man to die from hard work, but I have known a lot who have died from worry. Take comfort in God's Word:

Be careful for nothing: but in every thing by prayer and supplication with thanksgiving let your requests be made known unto God.

—Philippians 4:6 KJV

Don't fret or worry. Instead of worrying, pray. Let petitions and praises shape your worries into prayers, letting God know your concerns. Before you know it, a sense of God's wholeness, everything coming together for good, will come and settle you down. It's wonderful what happens when Christ displaces worry at the center of your life.

—Philippians 4:6–7 MSG

Maturity eliminates fear. Don't worry about anything. The Lord's nearness leads Paul to forbid his readers from worrying. The solution to undue anxiety is prayer in everything, "in any matter of life." The way to be free of anxiety is to be prayerful about everything. While God is eager to hear our requests, they are to be accompanied with thanksgiving.

Cast thy burden upon the LORD, and he shall sustain thee: he shall never suffer the righteous to be moved.

—Psalm 55:22 KJV

Cast your cares on the LORD and he will sustain you; he will never let the righteous be shaken.

—Psalm 55:22 NIV

God invites us to burden Him with what burdens us. The psalm is a prayer by one who is being unjustly harassed and who has been betrayed by a friend. The entire Psalm 55 contains a prayer of petition, a lament over the man's present woeful state, and an expression of trust in God (verse 22).

When I am afraid, I will trust you.

—Psalm 56:3 NCV

What time I am afraid, I will trust in thee.

—Psalm 56:3 KJV

Trusting God's faithfulness dispels our fearfulness. Psalm 56 is a confident prayer for help.

Making the Transition from Staff to Supervisor

Have you recently been promoted to a new position as a manager or supervisor? As a first-time supervisor, you may feel overwhelmed by all of your new responsibilities, anxious about the transition, and stressed out about moving from "coworker" to "boss." Maybe you are concerned about the way others will react to your new status … about keeping up with a tougher workload … and wondering how to handle the new tasks you will be faced with, including hiring, disciplinary action, and even firing. You may be concerned with having to:

- Deal with co-workers who are jealous or resentful
- Earn the trust and respect of team members, peers, and superiors
- Delegate without making others feel as if they are being taken advantage of
- Master organizational skills essential for managers
- Use praise to reward and motivate
- Think like a leader instead of a follower
- Identify your personal roadblocks to leadership success, and rid yourself of them forever
- Take on a new position of authority *without* coming across as bossy, smug, or domineering
- Recognize and manage the different work/personality styles of your employees
- Improve your communication skills—essential for every effective manager

Basic Supervision: Learn Effective Leadership Skills to Maximize Employee Performance

As a supervisor, you are the one in charge, but you know all too well that your job description does not even begin to cover the many roles you actually fill. In today's world, supervisors and their teams have more complex relationships than ever before. A supervisor must be a friend, coach, boss, and mediator. You are responsible for:

- Delegating
- Motivating and praising
- Delivering criticism and discipline
- Working under pressure

- Meeting tight deadlines
- Training new employees
- Organizing people, projects, and schedules

Again and again, day after day!

<u>Source:</u> Fred Pryor Seminars, www.pryor.com

NOTES:

_____

_____

_____

_____

Avoiding the Basic Mistakes

Relax, meditate upon God's Word, make great strides to avoid these basic mistakes throughout your day, and learn the valuable lessons associated with each:

Basic Mistake #1—EXPECT SOMEBODY ELSE TO REDUCE YOUR STRESS
<u>Lesson</u>: Put *yourself* in charge of managing the pressure.

Basic Mistake #2—DECIDE NOT TO CHANGE
<u>Lesson</u>: People waste far more emotional energy desperately hanging on to old habits and beliefs than it would take for them to embrace the changes.

Basic Mistake #3—ACT LIKE A VICTIM
<u>Lesson</u>: Accept fate, and move on. You are better off if you appear resilient and remain productive.

Basic Mistake #4—TRY TO PLAY A NEW GAME BY THE OLD RULES
<u>Lesson</u>: Don't try harder, try differently.

Basic Mistake #5—SHOOT FOR THE LOW-STRESS WORK SETTING
<u>Lesson</u>: Don't fall into the trap of believing there's such a thing as a low-stress organization that is on track to survive.

Basic Mistake #6—TRY TO CONTROL THE UNCONTROLLABLE
<u>Lesson</u>: It is a bad investment of our psychological energy.

Basic Mistake #7—CHOOSE YOUR OWN PACE OF CHANGE
<u>Lesson</u>: Keep in step with the organization's intended rate of change.

Basic Mistake #8—FAIL TO ABANDON THE EXPENDABLE
<u>Lesson</u>: Eliminate unnecessary steps, get rid of busywork, and unload activities that don't contribute enough to the organization's current goals.

Basic Mistake # 9—SLOW DOWN
<u>Lesson</u>: Speed up. Cover more ground. Put your faith in action.

Basic Mistake #10—BE AFRAID OF THE FUTURE
<u>Lesson</u>: The best insurance policy for tomorrow is to make the most productive use of today.

Basic Mistake #11—PICK THE WRONG BATTLES
<u>Lesson</u>: Pick battles big enough to master, small enough to win.

In his book entitled, *Don't Sweat the Small Stuff at Work*, Dr. Richard Carlson articulates that we must accept the fact that there will always be someone mad at us at any given time during the workday. He says:

> *This is a difficult concept to accept, particularly if you are a "people pleaser," or worse still, an approval seeker. Yet I've found that if you don't make peace with this virtual inevitability, it guarantees that you will spend a great deal of time struggling with one of the unfortunate realities of life—disappointment.*
>
> *The fact that someone is virtually always going to be mad or at least disappointed in you is evitable because while you're busy trying to please one person, you're often disappointing someone else. Even if your intentions are entirely pure and positive, you simply can't be in two places at the same time. So, if two or more people want, need, or expect something from you—and you can't do it all—someone is going to be left disappointed. When you have dozens or even hundreds of demands on your time, and requests being fired at you from all different directions, a certain number of balls are going to be dropped. Mistakes are going to be made.*

From the errors of others, a wise man corrects his own.

NOTES:

_____

_____

_____

_____

Plan Your Steps Wisely

Up to forty percent of federal workers may retire by the year 2015. It is now that you realize that something bigger awaits you on the other side of the horizon. There are more complex jobs that you can handle. You have demonstrated an ability to learn, grow, develop, and to handle important situations in a mature manner. Promotion appears imminent. It is now time to *walk in what you now know*. For starters, recognize and acknowledge that in this society, the success of a company is directly tied to its ability to generate revenue. In 2002, nine of the eleven ten largest public companies in the world were based in the United States:

Company	Market Value
General Electric	$245,254B
Microsoft	$235,266B
Wal-Mart Stores	$217,771B
Exxon Mobil	$215,562B
Pfizer	$179,624B
Johnson & Johnson	$160,906B
BP (UK)	$150,164B
Citigroup	$150,057B
American International Group	$142,805B
Royal Dutch/Shell (Netherlands/UK)	$142,151B
Coca-Cola	$119,052B

Source: *The Wall Street Journal* Market Data Group.

Notice in the table that follows how the trend changed by the year 2012. The term "global leading company" gives a tough outlook especially in the modern competitive world. Business is not every one's cup of coffee due to the requirement of certain trading techniques. Adapting new ways of doing things, appreciation, and a genuine sense of commitment are the accelerating factors towards a company's success. An uncountable number of industries is spread across the universe but very few notable one's have their names engraved on the pages of accomplishment. Given below are the names of those fortunate few whose achievements are talked about throughout.

In 2012, only five of the ten largest public companies in the world are based in the United States as follows:

Company	Market Value
Exxon Mobil	$407.4B
JPMorgan Chase	$170.1B
General Electric	$213.7B
Royal Dutch Shell	$227.6B
Industrial and Commercial Bank of China	$237.2B
HSBC Holdings	$164.3B

Company	Market Value
PetroChina	$294.7B
Berkshire Hathaway	$202.2B
Wells Fargo	*not posted*
Petróleo Brasil (or Petrobras)	$180.0B

Source: http://www.toptenofcity.com/commerce/top-10-largest-public-companies-in-the-world-2012.html

In *The 1992–2005 Job Outlook in Brief*, published by United States Department of Labor, Bureau of Labor Statistics, it was predicted that significant job growth would occur in certain career fields over a fifteen-year period. While some predictions have come to fruition, others have not for a variety of reasons. The predictions for the higher percentage change in various fields were as follows:

Executive, Administrative, and Managerial Occupations
Construction contractors and managers	47%

Professional Specialty Occupations
Metallurgical, ceramic, and materials engineers	28%

- **Computer, mathematical, and operations research occupations**
  - Computer scientists and systems analysts — 111%
- **Life sciences**
  - Lawyers and judges — 28%
- **Social scientists and urban planners**
  - Psychologists — 48%
- **Social and recreation workers**
  - Human services workers — 136%
- **Teachers, librarians, and counselors**
  - School teachers (K, elementary, and Secondary) — 34%
- **Health Diagnosing Occupations**
  - Podiatrists — 37%
- **Health Assessment and treating occupations**
  - Physical therapists — 88%
- **Communications Occupations**
  - Public relations specialists — 26%
  - Reports and correspondents — 26%
- **Visual arts occupations**
  - Photographers and camera operators — 25%
- **Performing arts occupations**
  - Actors, directors, producers — 54%

Technicians and Related Support Occupations
Radiologic technologists	63%

- **Technicians except health**
  - Paralegals — 86%

Marketing and Sales Occupations
Travel agents	66%

Administrative Support Occupations, Including Clerical
Teacher aides	43%

Service Occupations
- **Protection service occupations**
  Correction officers 70%
- **Food and beverage preparation**
  Chefs, cooks, and other kitchen workers 38%
- **Health service occupations**
  Medical assistants 71%
- **Personal service and cleaning occupations**
  Homemaker-Home health aides 136%

Agriculture, Forestry, Fishing, and Related Occupations
Fishers, hunters, and trappers 5%

Mechanics, Installers, and Repairers
Automotive body repairers 30%

Construction Trades and Extractive Occupations
Insulation workers 40%

Production Occupations
- **Assemblers**
  Blue-collar worker supervisors 12%
- **Food procession occupations**
  Butchers and meat, poultry, and fish cutters 3%
- **Metalworking and plastics-working occupations**
  Jewelers 19%
- **Plant and systems operators**
  Water and wastewater treatment plant operators 18%
- **Printing occupations**
  Printing press operators 20%
- **Textile, apparel, and furnishings occupations**
  Upholsterers 11%
- **Miscellaneous production occupations**
  Ophthalmic laboratory technicians 22%

Transportation and Material Moving Occupations
Truck drivers 26%

Handlers, Equipment Cleaners, Helpers, and Laborers ... 17%

If there is a way to achieve greatness, it can be done. Your talent is God's gift to you. What you do with it is your gift back to God.

Every good gift and every perfect gift is from above, and cometh down from the Father of lights, with whom is no variableness, neither shadow of turning.

—James 1:17 KJV

Every good gift and every perfect gift is from above, and comes down from the Father of lights, with whom there is no variation or shadow of turning.

—James 1:17 NKJV

Recognize and acknowledge the following: God is the Father, or Creator, of the heavenly bodies; As our Creator, He is certainly more stable than us. With God, there is no change and He is immutable; God is only good. This last principle relates to verse 17.

For do I now persuade men, or God? Or do I seek to please men? For if I yet pleased men, I should not be the servant of Christ.

—Galatians 1:10 KJV

Be a servant of Christ, do not try to please men:

Never allow somebody else's approval to become your goal. Don't try to prove to them that you are valuable. They may never see your good qualities. To deal effectively with others, you must be able to work alongside them—without allowing yourself to be controlled by their moods, or governed by their opinion of you.

Observe people who are good at their work—skilled workers are always in demand and admired; they don't take a backseat to anyone.

—Proverbs 22:29 MSG

Seest thou a man diligent in his business? He shall stand before kings; he shall not stand before mean men.

—Proverbs 22:29 KJV

Hard workers get rich. Skilled workers are always in demand and admired. For example, Nehemiah started out as a waiter, but ended up rebuilding the whole city of Jerusalem.

And they that be wise shall shine as the brightness of the firmament; and they that turn many to righteousness as the stars forever and ever.

—Daniel 12:3 KJV

The wise people will shine like the brightness of the sky. Those who teach others to live right will shine like stars forever and ever.

—Daniel 12:3 NCV

Allow your *light* to shine brightly as a means to "attract" others toward the goodness of God Almighty!

_____

_____

_____

_____

Workplace Information to Know

Federal Workers Get Gloomier About Jobs

In 2011, a front-page *Washington Post* newspaper article titled "Survey finds decline in satisfaction for first time in four Years," by Ed O'Keefe, highlighted a common theme in the workplace. Satisfaction among federal workers is down for the first time in four years, according to an annual survey of government agencies that ranks attitudes about everything from agency leaders to workplace culture. Concerns about pay, leadership, and department's missions are the main factors behind the growing gloom.

Best-Ranked Workplaces (top large agencies on a 1-to-100 scale)

1. Federal Deposit Insurance Corporation   85.9

2. Nuclear Regulatory Commission   79.1

3. Government Accountability Office   78.9

4. Smithsonian Institution   76.0

5. NASA   72.5

Source: *Washington Post* newspaper, Front Page, November 16, 2011.

What Employers Monitor in the Workplace

The most common ways employers check up on their employees:

- Monitor Internet use—21%
- Review e-mail—16%
- Eavesdrop on phone conversations—13%
- Monitor use of online training program—8%
- Record phone conversations—6%
- Review voice mail—5%
- Video—4%

Source: Haralson, Darryl and Quin Tian, *Sales & Marketing Management* magazine survey of 500 executives, *USA TODAY* SNAPSHOTS®.

Ghost Work

"Ghost work" is a term that refers to the extra work required by staff during an economic downturn. Many executives face difficult challenges during these times, managing the leaner, demoralized staffs that remain after layoffs and cost-cutting. They still have to get the same amount of work done despite the shrinking staff and resources.

Inevitably, these bosses have to ask their employees to do not only their regular jobs but also the work of axed colleagues—and without additional pay. The result is that no one gets the training needed to do this ghost work, or the jobs of departed colleagues. The problem with ghost work is that employees not only have more work to do but aren't very efficient at it since they may not have the knowledge they need to do it well. The only option is to work smarter.

The work that ghost work employees must do makes them feel less than grateful to survive job cuts. From the boss' point of view, the survivors are supposed to feel lucky that they have jobs, but instead they feel they're working harder than ever—and they need attention, encouragement, and help.

Source: Hymowitz, Carol, *The Wall Street Journal*, Marketplace Section, "Getting a Lean Staff to Do 'Ghost Work' of Departed Colleagues," October 22, 2002.

NOTES:

_____

_____

_____

_____

Test Your Stress Level

Circle all of the events that have occurred in your life over the past twelve to eighteen months. Total your **Life Change Units** (LCUs). LCUs in bold are specific to the workplace.

1.	Death of spouse	100
2.	Divorce	73
3.	Marital separation	65
4.	**Jail term**	63
5.	Death of a close family member	63
6.	Personal injury or illness	53
7.	Marriage	50
8.	**Fired from job**	47
9.	Marital reconciliation	45
10.	**Retirement**	45
11.	Change in health of a family member	44
12.	Pregnancy	40

13.	Sex difficulties	39
14.	Gain of new family member	39
15.	**Business readjustment**	39
16.	**Change in financial state**	38
17.	Death of close friend	37
18.	**Change to different line of work**	36
19.	Change in the number of arguments with spouse	35
20.	Loan for major purchase	31
21.	Foreclosure of loan/mortgage	30
22.	**Change in responsibilities at work**	29
23.	Son or daughter leaving home	29
24.	Trouble with in-laws	29
25.	**Outstanding personal achievement**	28
26.	**Spouse begins or stops work**	26
27.	Begin or end school	26
28.	**Change in living conditions**	25
29.	**Revision of personal habits**	24
30.	**Trouble with boss**	23
31.	**Change in work hours or conditions**	20
32.	**Change in residence**	20
33.	Change in schools	20
34.	Change in recreation	19
35.	Change in church activities	19
36.	Change in social activities	18
37.	Loan for a lesser purchase	17
38.	Change in sleeping habits	16
39.	Change in number of family get-togethers	15
40.	Change in eating habits	15
41.	**Vacation**	13
42.	Holidays	12
43.	Minor violations of the law	11

Calculating your Results

0—150 LCUs: Your level of stress based on life change is *low*

150—300 LCUs: *Borderline* stress level—you should attempt to minimize changes in your life at this time

Over 300 CLUs: Your stress levels are *high*—you should minimize changes in your life and institute some stress intervention techniques.

Source: American Massage Therapy Association brochure

Questions for Personal Reflection or Group Discussion

1. *Applying What You Now Know* is a term that means what to you?

   _____

   _____

   _____

2. How did you rate your stress level? How would you determine its relevancy to your current status at work?

   _____

   _____

   _____

3. How has God's Word prepared you for your present position in the workplace?

   _____

   _____

   _____

4. What steps will you take to avoid the basic mistakes in the workplace?

   _____

   _____

   _____

5. How have you handled your transition from the formative years to the journeyman years? Cite some examples.

   _____

   _____

   _____

food for thought

ON APPLYING WHAT YOU KNOW

I Now Know That:

1. During the early 1900s, 85% of our workers were in agriculture. Now agriculture involves less than 3% of the workforce.
2. In 1950, 73% of U.S. employees worked in production or manufacturing. Now less than 15% do.
3. The Department of Labor estimated that by the year 2000 at least 44% of all workers would be in data services (gathering, processing, retrieving, or analyzing information).
4. Careers come and go. Jobs change. This is nothing new—it is just happening far faster than ever before.
5. Work is going global. We have entered the *Information Age*. The economy is shifting more and more toward *services*, and toward *knowledge work*. Knowledge has become our most important "product."
6. The world does not care about our opinions or our feelings. The world rewards only those of us who catch on to what's happening, who invest our energy in finding and seizing the opportunities brought about by change.
7. In 1991, for the first time ever, companies spent more money on computing and communications gear than the combined monies spent on industrial, mining, farm, and construction equipment.
8. Since 1983, the U.S. work world has added 25 million computers. The number of cellular telephone subscribers has jumped from zero in 1983 to 16 million by the end of 1993.
9. Communication technology is radically changing the speed, direction, and amount of information flow, even as it alters work roles all across organizations. As a case in point, the number of secretaries is down 521,000 just since 1987.
10. A weekday edition of *The New York Times* contains more information than the average person was likely to come across in a lifetime during seventeenth-century England.
11. Today's average consumers wear more computing power on their wrists than existed in the entire world before 1961.
12. During the decade of the 1980s, a total of 230 companies—46%—disappeared from the "Fortune 500." Obviously, size does not guarantee continued success. Neither does a good reputation.

Chapter Five

Become What You Have Learned

"You can get everything in life you want if you will just help other people get want they want!"

—*Zig Ziglar* (1926–2012)
World renowned motivational speaker

Be devoted to one another in love. Honor one another above yourselves. Never be lacking in zeal, but keep your spiritual fervor, serving the Lord. Be joyful in hope, patient in affliction, faithful in prayer.

—Romans 12:10–12 NIV

Be kindly affectioned one to another with brotherly love; in honour preferring one another; Not slothful in business; fervent in spirit; serving the Lord; Rejoicing in hope; patient in tribulation; continuing in prayer.

—Romans 12:10–12 KJV

Cultivate your skills with patience.
Be fair and cordial as you progress.

*D*r. Robert H. Schuller started a church in 1955 with 100 members in a drive-in theater. Today, he runs a multi-million member ministry and can be seen on a weekly worldwide broadcast entitled, "*Hour of Power*." From his boyhood on a poor Iowa farm, he became a counselor to United States Presidents and an inspiring voice to millions. Even though he was born in a house at the dead end of a dirt road that had no name and no number, Dr. Schuller challenges us all to become what we have learned through his inspiring words—"*If you can dream it, you can do it.*"

In his book, *My Journey*, Dr. Schuller gives an account of his humble beginnings. His journey began in a home with no electricity and no proper running water. After graduating from college and entering Western Theological Seminary, he realized that as long as you have a burning desire and a dream, you can go anywhere from nowhere. In the book, Dr. Schuller recalls that on September 14, 1980, a donated organ's music filled the space of the world's largest all-glass auditorium—the Crystal Cathedral.[6]

We are Responsible and Accountable to God

Small kindnesses, small courtesies, small considerations, habitually practiced in our social intercourse give a greater charm to the character than the display of great talents and accomplishments

—Mary Ann Kelly

The people who make a difference in your life are *not* the ones with the most credentials, the most money, or the most awards. They are the ones who *care*. God's Word says, "*But the path of the just is as the shining light, that shineth more and more unto the perfect day*" (Proverbs 4:18). Effective teaching comes only through a changed person. When you stop changing, you stop leading. Because the Apostle Paul was forced to spend all but seven years of his ministry in prison, we get to read his life-changing epistles 2000 years later. His work attests to the fact that the greatest risk of all is to risk nothing.

"If not you, who? If not now, when?"
—ABRAHAM MASLOW

Responsibility

One of the most popular scriptures in *The Holy Bible* describes the awesome principle of stewardship and responsibility. " *... For unto whomsoever much is given, of him shall be much required: and to whom men have committed much, of him they will ask the more,*" as found in the book of Luke (12:48). It stresses the heavy responsibility of servants, as followers of Jesus are supposed to be. The

---

[6] Schuller, Robert H. "If you can dream it, you can do it," *Parade* magazine, October, 21, 2001. pgs.14–16.

word responsibility represents the state, quality, or fact of being responsible. It is derived from two words—response and ability. It is a measure of our ability to respond to a given situation, circumstance, or stewardship. Jesus teaches us a valuable lesson about responsibility in verses 41 through 48. He teaches that the faithful and wise steward is blessed and will be made a ruler over all that he has. The unfaithful servant, however, is punished in four ways:

- The Lord will not look for him,
- He will cut him into two,
- He will appoint his portion with the unbelievers, and
- Shall be beaten with many stripes!

But He that knew not, and did commit things worthy of stripes, shall be beaten with few stripes. For unto whomsoever much is given, of him shall be much required: and to whom men have committed much, of him they will ask the more.

—Luke12:48 KJV

The servant who knows what his master wants and ignores it, or insolently does whatever he pleases, will be thoroughly thrashed. But if he does a poor job through ignorance, he'll get off with a slap on the hand. Great gifts mean great responsibilities; greater gifts, greater responsibilities!

—Luke 12:47–48 MSG

But you, man of God, run away from all those things. Instead, live in the right way, serve God, have faith, love, patience, and gentleness.

—1 Timothy 6:11 NCV

But thou, O man of God, flee these things; and follow after righteousness, godliness, faith, love, patience, meekness.

—1 Timothy 6:11 KJV

Flee these things means shun a love for money (verse 10) and the striving for material wealth with all of their resulting woes. *Follow after* means pursue. Righteousness is practical correctness, conforming to God's will in our thinking and acting. Godliness is proper reverence—fear—for, and obedience to, God. Faith is a trust in God that grows stronger. Love is a maturing affection for God and man. Patience is perseverance or steadfastness in life and service. Meekness is power under control, or gentleness.

We are entrusted with a high degree of responsibility as Christians. We are "Christ-like ones"—*christos*—ambassadors for Christ, and are instructed to be living epistles. God trusts that we will fulfill the purpose for which we were born and carry out His mandate, " ... *to seek and to save that which was lost.*" Where we work is prime territory to win souls for Christ. New opportunities are presented to us daily to demonstrate the love of Christ. We are the substance of things hoped for and the evidence that there is a God in which people cannot see. We should greet all people each morning with a big smile and a gesture of "Good Morning!" Allow the love of the Lord to be visible throughout the workday. Take your responsibility seriously. Win souls for Christ while earning an honest day's wage. The following scriptures are God's plan for us to obey, adhere, and implement in our lives:

And the LORD said unto Cain, Where is Abel thy brother? And he said, I know not: Am I my brother's keeper?

—Genesis 4:9 KJV

Then the Lord said to Cain, "Where is your brother Abel?" "I don't know," he replied. "Am I my brother's keeper?"

—Genesis 4:9 NIV

Rescue those who are unjustly sentenced to die; save them as they stagger to their death. Don't excuse yourself by saying, "Look, we didn't know." For God understands all hearts, and he sees you. He who guards your soul knows you knew. He will repay all people as their actions deserve.

—Proverbs 24:11–12 NLT

If thou forbear to deliver them that are drawn unto death, and those that are ready to be slain; If thou sayest, Behold, we knew it not, doth not he that pondereth the heart consider it? And he that keepeth thy soul, doth not he know it? And shall not he render to every man according to his works?

—Proverbs 24:11–2 KJV

But he that is an hireling, and not the shepherd, whose own the sheep are not, seeth the wolf coming, and leaveth the sheep, and fleeth: and the wolf catcheth them, and scattereth the sheep. The hireling fleeth, because he is an hireling, and careth not for the sheep.

—John 10:12–13 KJV

I am the Good Shepherd. The Good Shepherd puts the sheep before himself, sacrifices himself if necessary. A hired man is not a real shepherd. The sheep mean nothing to him. He sees a wolf come and runs for it, leaving the sheep to be ravaged and scattered by the wolf. He's only in it for the money. The sheep don't matter to him.

—John 10:12–13 MSG

And when they opposed themselves, and blasphemed, he shook his raiment, and said unto them, Your blood be upon your own heads; I am clean: from henceforth I will go unto the Gentiles.

—Acts 18:6 KJV

But when they opposed and insulted him, Paul shook the dust from his clothes and said, "Your blood is upon your own heads—I am innocent. From now on I will go preach to the Gentiles."

—Acts 18:6 NLT

And so each of us shall give an account of himself [give an answer in reference to judgment] to God.

—Romans 14:12 AMP

So then every one of us shall give account of himself to God.

—Romans 14:12 KJV

Each person must be responsible for himself.

—Galatians 6:5 NCV

For every man shall bear his own burden.

—Galatians 6:5 KJV

But if anyone does not provide for his own, and especially for those of his household, he has denied the faith and is worse than an unbeliever.

—1 Timothy 5:8 NKJV

But if any provide not for his own, and especially for those of his own house, he hath denied the faith, and is worse than an infidel.

—1 Timothy 5:8 KJV

Accountability

Accountability means to be responsible *and* answerable. With such an awesome responsibility of representing God in the earth through Jesus Christ, we will be held accountable for our actions as well as inactions. Accountability is derived from two words—*account* and *ability*. It signifies a willingness to accept the outcome of which we have been trusted to manage, oversee, or care for in general. In a sense, responsibility and accountability are inseparable. In the original Greek translation, accountability is derived from the word *kataxioō*, or account, and it denotes "to account worthy" or "to judge worthy" as referenced in Luke 20:35 and 21:36. This verb is actually taken from two Greek words—*kata*—meaning "intensive" and—*axios*—meaning "worthy." Another translation for the word account comes from—*katischuō*—and means "to prevail" (Acts 5:41) and "were counted worthy" (2 Thessalonians 1:5).

As we progress on our respective jobs, we are held to a higher standard concerning our overall responsibility. Likewise, the accountability factor stiffens and the expectations increase. During the early years in our careers, we spend time learning about the new job and how to function within the team setting. Expectations are not unreasonably high at this point in time. But as we move into the next phase—team leader, manager, or senior analyst—we are held to a higher standard and higher accountability. It is expected that we will apply those things that we have learned through on-the-job training. Results that can be measured are now expected with minimal oversight. We will be accountable for the results, either positively or negatively. Knowing this, Christians have a dual role on the job—to represent God according to His Word *and* to be excellent workers on the job. As we let our *light* so shine before men, we are obeying God's commandment and He will make provisions for us to excel in and on our jobs. We are, in essence, entrusted to raise the level of productivity of others around us. He will continually protect us from man's evil devices. He will strategically place the right people in our paths and open doors.

Upon further examination of the root word account, it means to reckon, calculate, consider, let your mind dwell on, and give reasons for. God's Word describes it as accepting responsibility for in Matthew 12:36, Luke 16:2, and Romans 14:12. When someone is accounted, it is credited to or recognized as belonging to someone as referenced in Galatians 3:6 and Luke 22:24. Also, an account is a detailed record, count, or credit as referenced in Deuteronomy 2:11 and Psalm 144:3.

Blessed is the man whose strength is in thee; in whose heart are the ways of them.

—Psalm 84:5 KJV

Blessed is the man whose strength is in You, Whose heart is set on pilgrimage.

—Psalm 84:5 NKJV

Be strong in the Lord while considering the concerns of others before your own.

Become What You Desire to See in Others

Ever hear of Edcouch, Elsa, or La Villa, Texas? In these tiny towns, 90% of the households have incomes of less than $10,000, and 91% of parents lack a high school diploma. Yet, in the last decade, Edcouch-Elsa High School has sent forty-five students to elite colleges and universities such as Stanford, Brown, Yale, and Princeton, while 65% of graduating students go on to some form of higher education—well above national norms for Hispanic students. More remarkable, many graduates choose to return to these towns to live, work, and encourage others to achieve their goals. This commitment has been nurtured by a movement called "place-based education," which takes the history, culture, economy, and ecology of a community and uses them as both a textbook and laboratory. Thus, the community becomes a classroom. Mr. Francisco "Frank" Guarjardo, a history teacher who helped found The Llano Grande Center at the high school says, "Our students don't inherit yachts, stores, or stock options, but they live in a vibrant community with a wealth of human stories."

Today, communities across the nation are applying the place-based education techniques to teach a broad range of subjects, including science, history, geography, the arts, and even math in more than 700 rural elementary and secondary schools in thirty-three states, as follows:

Clinton and Jackson, Louisiana	Students analyzed water samples from creeks to determine the flow of pollutants.
Mendocino, California	Students restored a Chinese temple.
Sante Fe, New Mexico	Students interviewed Pueblo tribal elders about traditional growing cycles and plant remedies.
In 18 rural schools in Vermont	Students worked with community members to solve local problems.

Source: *"When the Community is a Classroom," Parade* Magazine, April 28, 2002, pg. 8.

Conversely, Apple Chief Executive Tim Cook received compensation for 2011 worth $378 million, one of the biggest pay packages on record, boosted by restricted stock awards that he will receive throughout the coming decade (2010–2020). What community-based programs do you believe that Apple promotes?

Source: *Washington Post*, Business, January 15, 2012.

A one man mission of mercy

Every Sunday at 1:30 PM, rain or shine, Hector Perez can be found in the parking lot of the Bound Brook, New Jersey train station. Members of about thirty indigent families, most of them Hispanic immigrants, stand in line waiting for him. Without question, Mr. Perez provides bags of food and used clothes for the needy. The only requirement is that they sign their names in a notebook, proving that they received Mr. Perez's help. He is not affiliated with any agencies such as the Red Cross or Salvation Army, or any church outreach groups that already serve the impoverished. Instead, he recognized the need of those who do not have transportation to the neighboring towns' food bank and chose to get involved after hurricane Floyd devastated the town in 1999. He delivered food from the food bank to flood victims and brought overstocked food from churches back to the food bank. Mr. Perez, who is unemployed, became disabled when he injured his right arm while working at a plastics factory in Plainfield, New Jersey twenty-five years ago. "God gave me enough strength and the will do this, so I am here," he said. "If I don't show up, then all these people have no food."

Source: Bugman, Cathy, "No One Goes Hungry If He Can Help It," *Sunday Star Ledger*, June 9, 2002.

Souper Bowl vs. Super Bowl

While many Americans are thinking about an evening in front of the television watching the most highly anticipated football game of the year, a number of teenagers across the country will be marking Super Bowl Sunday in a different way. In the morning before the kickoff, Souper Bowl of Caring, an annual event that began thirteen years ago in Columbia, South Carolina, starts its day with approximately 15,000 congregations across the country raising money for food pantries, soup kitchens, and other local efforts to help the disadvantaged. In New Jersey, for example, First Baptist Church in Westfield asked each of its members to throw a dollar into the soup pots, resulting in $300 to $400 in donation for the Community Food Bank of New Jersey. Not far away, fifteen or twenty volunteers from the youth group of Connecticut Farms Presbyterian Church in Union stand in the entry after their 11:00 AM service to accept cash donations and non-perishable foods for the food pantry at their church. At St. John Neumann Roman Catholic Church Parish in Califon, junior high schoolers take responsibility for the Souper Bowl of Caring. As they remind the parishioners of this project, they collect money and cans of soup. The soup is donated to a program that the teens choose as does the approximate $550. The students personally deliver the soup to a soup kitchen and spend a day volunteering sometime in February or March. Crescent Avenue Presbyterian Church in Plainfield said that the money collected during Souper Bowl of Caring goes to the bag lunch program at the church, which feeds thirty-six people per day, five days per week. The high school youth group at St. Stephen's Lutheran Church in Edison collects their donations. The money raised, which could be as much as $200, goes to the Lutheran World Hunger drive. Says Pastor Anna Kalandova, *"I think it's a good project for American kids. We want to involve them in social ministry."*

Information on the Souper Bowl of Caring is available at: www.souperbowl.org or 1 (800) 358-7687

Source: Turner, Patricia C. "Hunger Drives Them," *Sunday Star Ledger*, January 19, 2003.

_____

_____

_____

_____

Seven Billion

The human population will hit seven billion today, the U.N. has declared. A week-old baby (Aria Amour Hill), born in the District (Washington, DC, USA) on October 23, 2011, at Washington Hospital Center, enters a world population that is aging more rapidly than experts expected. How will aging societies cope with fewer workers for every retiree?

In this *Washington Post* column titled, "A World Growing—and Growing Grayer," life expectancy at birth in Africa, North America, Oceania, Europe, Latin America, and Asia, representing the world population, averages eighty-plus years of age by the year 2050.

In far better shape demographically is the United States, with a fertility rate just slightly below replacement level. Immigration boosts the workforce. But the baby-boom generation is storming the higher age brackets; the number of Americans aged sixty to sixty-four jumped from 11 million to 17 million in the most recent census. When Social Security was established in 1935, life expectancy in the United States was just under sixty-two years at birth. Today, it is seventy-eight and rising.

The aging of the world will change cultures in myriad ways. People may have to extend their working lives far beyond the traditional retirement age. Countries may start competing for immigrants. Across the planet, vast numbers of people already are migrating from high-fertility countries to those that need workers.

The planet as a whole does not have a baby shortage. Every minute of every day, according to the Population Reference Bureau, the number of births exceeds the number of deaths by 158. But the growth is not spread evenly. Of the net increase, 154 are in the developing world.

Ethiopia and Germany have roughly the same population today, but Ethiopia's is expected to more than double in the next four decades while Germany's is projected to shrink by 10 million people.

The demographic transition is a significant factor in the financial crisis in Europe and the on-going debt debate in the United States. In both places, the number of workers will steadily and dramatically decrease in relation to retirees. In the United States, the ratio of working-age people to retirement-age people will go from about 5-to-1 to 3-to-1 in the next two decades, according to the Census Bureau.

Source: *Washington Post*, Monday, October 31, 2011, and United Nations Population Division, by Joel Achenbach.

Test Your "Common Sense"

Take this test as a means of measuring how you would handle certain situations or respond to certain circumstances. At the end of this test, you will be able to measure your level of *common sense* based upon a scoring system that measures Intelligence Quotient (IQ). Remember, this is only a test. IQ tests only measure where you are today. The IQ test is not an accurate measure of your potential! Do not allow the results of any test dictate your value or worth to God. You are fearfully and wonderfully made by Him and He loves you. You are only required to do what is pleasing in His sight and see yourself as God sees you. Everybody needs love. Always remember the lyrics of "*Jesus Loves Me*," written by Anna B. Warner (1824–1915). It is a popular song that is sung by children and adults around the world—"*Jesus loves me, this I know, for the Bible tells me so.*" The cross of Jesus is the supreme evidence of the love of God.

1. You are about to cross a busy intersection as you walk home, but the light is out of order. What should you do?
    a.   Cross with caution
    b.   Don't cross

2. Tuna is your favorite food, and you love all varieties equally. Today, you find the fancy grade on sale at half-price: Now it costs only twice as much as the unfancy grade. You're always short of cash. What should you do?
    a.   Buy the fancy kind.
    b.   Buy the unfancy kind.

3. You need a warm winter coat, and you've found two on sale. One is twice as warm as the other, but the other one looks much better. Which should you buy?
    a.   The warmer one.
    b.   The one that looks better.

4. You should get a haircut before you go on a job interview tomorrow, but you don't have enough money. What should you do?
    a.   Go to the interview.
    b.   Cancel the interview.

5. Your favorite shoes are wearing out. They can be repaired as good as new for $50. A new pair costs $100. What should you do?
    a.   Repair the shoes.
    b.   Buy a new pair.

6. You're starting to take a test. One of the directions notes that there is a penalty for guessing. What should you do?
    a.   Guess.
    b.   Don't guess.

7. You're looking for an apartment and find two that you can afford. One has a view of the park. The other has a view of a flashing neon sign. Which apartment should you rent?
    a.   The one with the park view.
    b.   The one with the view of the flashing neon sign.

Is Work Your God?

Ultimately, we are working for the *Lord*. He is the boss's Boss, the supervisor's Supervisor, and foreman's Foreman, and the manager's Manager. *"And whatsoever ye do, do it heartily, as to the Lord, and not unto men"* (Colossians 3:23). The goal of work is not to gain wealth and possessions, but to serve the common good and bring glory to God (Robert Foster). Contrary to the way we may feel sometimes, work itself is not a curse. When we learn to see it properly, we realize that in almost every job there is a way of working for and with God. We need to understand that the perfect life is not a work-free existence. Work was part of the Lord's blueprint for daily life in Paradise. When we accept God's perspective on work, we will find fulfillment.[7]

The ability to work is a wonderful gift, but are we taking it too far? There was a time, a generation ago, when people left their jobs at the office, but now we come home to e-mail and phone messages. God commands us in Exodus 20:3, *"You shall have no other gods before me."* No matter what our occupation, we must keep work in perspective. God and family are more important than dedication to a job. Work is a gift, not a god. Honor God with everything you have. Give Him the first and the best. In 1 Thessalonians 4:11–12, we are instructed to " *… study to be quiet, and to do your work with your own hands, as we commanded you. That ye may walk honestly toward them that are without, and that ye may have lack of nothing."* The goal is to win the respect of unbelievers. They need to see that your faith in Christ makes a positive difference in the practical, everyday aspects of your life. In the book of Titus, the Apostle Paul tells Titus that part of the motive workers should have is to *"make the teaching about God our Saviour attractive"* (2:10 NIV). An honest day's work backs up our profession of faith and points to the truth of the gospel. Ecclesiastes says that life is short, wealth is fleeting, and one's relationship with God and people is more important than any lesser concept of success. Likewise, in the book of Proverbs it teaches us *"Do not wear yourself out to get rich; have the wisdom to show restraint"* (23:4 NIV).

Dr. Dave Arnott, associate professor of management at Dallas Baptist University, says, "I do not know whether work is taking over family and community, or whether family and community are giving up their place to work. But I know the movement is going on. Everyone's job seems to be who they are." We tend to equate our identity with what we do for a living.

The president of the Families and Work Institute says, "How busy you are has become the red badge of courage … It has become a status symbol," even though people complain about it.[8] Our sense of personal worth is closely connected to a feeling that we are accomplishing something purposeful with our lives. Because of that, work and a satisfying life are inseparable. Unfortunately, work does not always give us that sense of satisfaction. Always remember—to show His love, Jesus died for us. To show our love, we must live for Him. Work for God, not man!

---

[7] RBC Ministries, *Our Daily Bread—How Can I Find Satisfaction in my Work?,* 1991 Grand Rapids, MI.
[8] RBC Ministries, *Our Daily Bread,* February 21, 2003.

Don't just make money, make an impact!

—Atty. Willie Gary

After all the complaints about how the workplace is never a meritocracy and how back-stabbers always win, now is the time for hard-working and trustworthy managers to present themselves as the new face of upper management.

With dozens of senior executives under scrutiny for wrongdoings, middle managers are "like kids in dysfunctional families," says Dory Hollander, a partner at WiseWorkplaces in Arlington, Virginia. "They're looking at the bosses they've depended on and saying, 'I don't want to be like them—and maybe I can do whole lot better.'"

Middle managers often have more regular contact with customers, suppliers, and employees than their top bosses, so they have a chance to show their integrity, the quality most desired in leaders today. Pat Cook, head of Cook & Co., a boutique executive search firm, says that during the dot-com boom, youth, speed, and exuberance were the most highly valued traits, but in the past few months clients mostly want to know they can trust a candidate.

"We're back to basics where what counts is honesty and reliability, along with the ability to get hard-core results," she says, "All those people who got ahead for all the wrong reasons are going to have to stand aside."[9]

NOTES:

_____

_____

_____

_____

It's Okay to Glorify God at Work

In the *Fortune* Magazine article by Marc Gunther entitled, "God & Business: Bringing spirituality into the workplace violates the old idea that faith and fortune don't mix. But a groundswell of believers is breaching the last taboo in corporate America," (July 9, 2001) the author encourages us to work from our soul. This article focuses on a group of executives, most of them Catholic, who belong to a Chicago-area group called Business Leaders of Excellence, Ethics, and Justice. For more than a decade they have wrestled with big questions: How can business promote family life? What is a just wage? When are layoffs justified?

"Spirituality in the workplace is exploding," declares Laura Nash, a senior research fellow at Harvard Business School who has followed the topic for a decade. The move is on to make the workplace a more ethical and humane arena, one where believers and nonbelievers alike can find

---

[9] Hymowitz, Carol, "Middle Managers Find Their Skills, Integrity Now Carry More Weight," *The Wall Street Journal*, Marketplace Section, July 30, 2002.

fulfillment. A similar article was published in 1953 by *Fortune* Magazine, entitled "Businessmen on Their Knees." The story noted that prayer groups were forming and that religious books were climbing up the bestseller lists, and asked, "Is it a superficial, merely utilitarian movement, or is it a genuinely spiritual awakening?" As Jose Zeilstra says, "Ultimately I am working for God. There is no higher calling than to serve God, and that does not mean only within the church. Ultimately, your life, whether it is work, family, or friends, is part of a larger plan."

The ongoing question remains: How do we treat the migrant worker, the single mother, and the illegal immigrant? These are the modern-day equivalents of the biblical poor.

Spiritual Revival at Work

The spiritual revival in the workplace reflects, in part, a broader religious reawakening in America, which remains one of the world's most observant nations. Depending on how the question is asked, as many as 95% of Americans say they believe in God. The Princeton Religious Research Index, which has tracked the strength of organized religion in America since World War II, reports a sharp increase in religious beliefs and practices since the mid-1990s. When the Gallup Poll asked Americans in 1999 if they felt a need to experience spiritual growth, 78% said yes, up from 20% in 1994. Sales of Bibles and prayer books, inspirational volumes, and books about philosophy and Eastern religions are growing faster than any other category, with the market expanding from $1.69 billion to about $2.24 billion in the past five years, according to the Book Industry Study Group.

Psalm 118:8, located in the center of *The Holy Bible*, reads, *"It is better to trust in the LORD than to put confidence in man."*

Leading Virtual Teams to Real Results

Here are some tips on how leaders are using social technologies to work virtually:

- Rich media, such as live virtual meetings, can make virtual interactions feel more realistic
- Frequent contact keeps connections to virtual workers fresh
- Mixing media, such as the use of forums, vlogs, blogs, and discussion groups allows people to interact in a style most comfortable to them
- Meeting face-to-face at least once helps create a bond that can be connected virtually
- Simple technologies, such as a personal phone call can help motivate a virtual worker, knowing they are not out of sight, out of mind

Source: Meister, Jeanne C. and Karie Willyerd, *Harvard Business Publishing.*

NOTES:

_____

_____

_____

_____

Questions for Personal Reflection or Group Discussion

1. Discuss some examples of how you have applied what you have learned as your career progressed.

   _____

   _____

   _____

2. Why is it okay to glorify God at work? What purpose does it serve?

   _____

   _____

   _____

3. Your IQ defines your intelligence at the time of the test. However, God knows your potential. Will you rely on the IQ test or God's plan for your life?

   _____

   _____

   _____

4. Service to others (Philippians 2:4) brings the ultimate fulfillment. How are you serving others in the workplace?

   _____

   _____

   _____

5. Accountability to God is what should drive your motivations. Are you living by that standard?

   _____

   _____

   _____

food for thought

ON LEARNING

People are successful not because of what they say, but because of what they ask.

—Attorney Johnnie L. Cochran, Jr.

Knowing is the enemy of learning . We've all got to be learners. Learners are people who are constantly questioning everything all the time, including, and with most difficulty, their own assumptions about what they know and what they don't know.

—Larry Wilson, founder and vice chairman,
Pecos River Division, AON Consulting

Seven reasons why questions stimulate learning:
1.   Questions demand answers.
2.   Questions stimulate thinking.
3.   Questions give us valuable information.
4.   Questions put you in control.
5.   Questions get people to open up.
6.   Questions lead to quality listening.
7.   Questions get people to persuade themselves.

<u>**Source:**</u> Leeds, Dorothy, The 7 Powers of Questions, Secrets to Successful Communication in Life and at Work.

Chapter Six

What Makes a Leader?

"All that is necessary for evil to triumph is for good men to do nothing."

—Edmund Burke,
January 9, 1795

*All of you are children of the **light**. You are children of the day. We don't belong to the night. We don't belong to the darkness. So let us not be like the others. They are asleep. Instead, let us be wide awake and in full control of ourselves.*

—1 Thessalonians 5:5–6 NIRV

*Ye are all children of **light**, and the children of the day: we are not of the night, nor of darkness. Therefore let us not sleep, as do others; but let us watch and be sober.*

—1 Thessalonians 5:5–6 KJV

Service to others makes you a great leader.

*Y*ou may be only one person in the world, but you may also be the world to one person (*Good Stuff*, January 2003). Our day's work is not done until we build up someone. God could send another flood, as He did in Noah's day, to cleanse away the wickedness of the world. He could, but He will not. He had promised never to do that again (Genesis 9:11). Instead, He chooses to work through human beings like us, changing us, and enabling us to function as His agents of change.

Only the one who has learned to *serve* is qualified to lead. A leader *is* a servant. Care and concern for others is a key attribute of a successful leader. Leadership is about capturing the imagination and enthusiasm of your people with clearly defined goals that cut through the fog like a beacon in the night. I have read and studied multiple books on leadership. All of the various sources lead to one common denominator—to be an effective leader, you must have followers. Christ-like leadership means considering the needs of our neighbors before our own, seeking their good, encouraging their spiritual growth and intimacy with God. It means treating others the way that God has treated us. Servant leaders employ gentle persuasion and reason rather than barking orders and ultimatums. Service for others is the basis of true greatness.

Leader, in its original Greek translation, has two meanings: *agō* and *hodēgeō*.

agō—"to bring, bear, carry, lead" is translated by the verb "to lead." The use of this version of "lead" is best captured in the following scriptures and is used metaphorically in Romans 2:4 (KJV emphasized).

*But when they shall **lead** you, and deliver you up, take no thought beforehand what ye shall speak, neither do ye premeditate: but whatsoever shall be given you in that hour, that speak ye: for it is not ye that speak, but the Holy Ghost.*

—Mark 13:11

*And Jesus being full of the Holy Ghost returned from Jordan, and was **led** by the Spirit into the wilderness.*

—Luke 4:1

Jesus was directed where to go at a predetermined time by the Holy Spirit

And he brought him into Jerusalem, and set him on a pinnacle of the temple, and said unto him, If thou be the Son of God, cast thyself down from hence.

—Luke 4:9

The higher parts of the temple stood next to a deep ravine. The elevation would have been considerable. Had Jesus performed this feat before the crowds below, He would certainly have attracted acclaim. But His aim remained obedience, not popularity.

*Then took they him, and **led** him, and brought him into the high priest's house. And Peter followed afar off.*

—Luke 22:54

*And the whole multitude of them arose, and **led** him into Pilate.*

—Luke 23:1

*And there were also two others, malefactors, **led** with him to be put to death.*

—Luke 23:32

*Then **led** they Jesus from Caiaphas unto the hall of judgment: and it was early; and they themselves went not into the judgment hall, lest they should be defiled; but that they might eat the passover.*

—John 18:28

*The place of the scripture which he read was this, HE WAS **LED** AS A SHEEP TO THE SLAUGHTER; AND LIKE A LAMB DUMB BEFORE HIS SHEARER, SO OPENED HE NOT HIS MOUTH.*

—Acts 8:32

*Or despiseth thou the riches of his goodness and forbearance and longsuffering; not knowing that the goodness of God **leadeth** thee to repentance?*

—Romans 2:4

The second meaning is *hodēgeō*—"to lead the way" and "guide" as used in Acts 1:16. It is used figuratively in the following scriptures:

... which was guide to them that took Jesus.

—Acts 1:16

*Let them alone: they be blinded leaders of the blind. And if the blind **lead** the blind, both shall fall into the ditch.*

—Matthew 15:14

Indicates ineffective leadership guides others to their ultimate destruction

Woe unto you, ye blind guides, which say, Whosoever shall swear by the temple, it is nothing; but whosoever shall swear by the gold of the temple, he is a debtor!

—Matthew 23:16

Ye blind guides, which strain at a gnat, and swallow a camel.

—Matthew 23:24

And art confident that thou thyself art a guide to the blind, a light of them which are in darkness.

—Romans 2:19

Seeking God's Will for Your Life

So you want to know what God has in mind for your life. You think, *If I only knew God's will, I would move full speed ahead.* You are not alone! All of us from time to time wonder what God would have us do.

Moses had it easy! That is, in discovering God's will, the stuttering fugitive could hardly miss the booming voice coming from a burning bush. Leading the Israelites out of Egypt was another matter.

God also had a pretty unique way for directing the apostle Paul. A blinding light knocked him to the ground. But at least Saul of Tarsus (Paul's name at the time) got the message. There, on the road to Damascus, blind and cowering on the ground, Jesus told him to "get up and go into the city, and you will be told what you must do" (Acts 9:6). Simply put, God wanted Paul to make a 180-degree turn and join the Christians he had been persecuting.

Then there's you. The lack of drama seems to indicate that God is leaving you to figure it all out on your own. But you're not entirely on your own. You have the Holy Spirit and the Bible.

Hearing from God

In order for your conscience to be reliable, it needs to be properly programmed, just like a computer. Anything found in the Bible comes with God's guarantee of authenticity. The nonnegotiable truth from scripture applies to everyone. The terms of God's general will are the same for you as they are for everyone else.

If you are serious about wanting to know God's will, faithfully explore God's Word. In addition to your daily time of reading the Bible, memorize verses and passages to hold in your heart. If you are having a down day, an uplifting verse may pop into your mind. Another passage may help you resist temptation. Think of scripture stored in your memory as your spiritual bank account.

Career Choices

Much of your life is built around your work. Whether you are seeking your first job or thinking about changing your career, a voice from a burning bush would be welcome, but do not expect it. While there's no blinding light involved in your career choice, it is not that God does not care. It is that He gives you the freedom to choose. As long as you are loyal to Him, He is happy with you becoming an accountant or working on the assembly line in a factory.

The psalmist wrote, "*You [God] created my inmost being; you knit me together in my mother's womb*" (Psalm 139:13). God gave you your talents and the passion to use them. His will is that you make the best use of these interests and abilities. What matters is not what job you do. What matters is that you choose a career that will allow you to bring the most glory to Him.

If your heart is pulling you in a certain direction (and this is not limited to work), there are other things you can do:

- Keep the matter in constant prayer.
- Seek counsel from your pastor or a mentor—someone you can trust to give you good and sound advice.
- Look for open or closed doors that might confirm God's leading, such as the sale of the home you now live in.

Source: Bailey, Esther, *Signs of the Times*, March 2013.

NOTES:

_____

_____

_____

_____

The Four Generations in the Workplace

For the first time in modern history, there are four generations of workers that report for duty to their respective workplaces each day. This revelation requires our immediate attention in terms of how we communicate, manage, lead, and instruct these four unique groups. Each group processes and retains information differently, thus, requiring distinguishing techniques to effective motivate them to become productive employees. These groups are known as: (1) The Traditional Generation, (2) Baby Boomers, (3) Gen Xers, and (4) The New Millennium. Characteristics that define each are listed below:

The Traditional Generation
(Born pre-1945)
- Train one-on-one
- Ask for their opinion
- Tell them their experiences are highly valued
- Do not forget to say "Please" and "Thank you"

Baby Boomers
(Born 1946–1964)
- Challenge them to create change
- Give public recognition
- Help them contribute to the greater good
- Show them where they can make a difference

The New Millennium
(Born post-1980)
- Provide frequent rewards
- Be clear about what rules are important and why
- Identify which rules you can bend, change, or get rid of
- Have some FUN!

Gen-Xer
(Born 1965–1980)
- Enable a balanced life
- Change represents opportunity
- Independent worker and learned
- Create a meritocracy

Source: MeaganJohnson.com

NOTES:

_____

_____

_____

_____

Lead God's Way

In his book, *The Eight Habits of the Heart*, Clifton Taulbert said the book's name is based upon the actions of his elders. The day-to-day community building during his youth in the Mississippi Delta, a place physically and spiritually quite distant from the big-city hallways of much of Corporate America, he found the eight habits to be timeless and universal and of immense value to organizations today. He specifically identified eight *Habits of the Heart*. I believe that Habit number six is pertinent to our day-to-day activities in the workplace. The Sixth Habit of the Heart is **HIGH EXPECTATIONS:**

> *Within the community, high expectations involve believing that others can be successful, telling them so, and praising their accomplishments.*

This demands that we do not abdicate to the daily routines of getting the job done; our role is lifting the sights of others and celebrating their success. In Glen Allen, people saw their visions for life extended through us, their children, grandchildren, and great-grandchildren. And this is the challenge of leadership today—to understand that the "vision" does stop at your door. Others must be welcomed and their gifts fully utilized.

Source: Leader to Leader, A Publication of the Leader to Leader Institute and Jossey-Bass, *Slow Down to Lead: Eight Principles for Building Strong Relationships,* by Clifton L. Taulbert, Number 49, Summer 2008.

Pastor John C. Maxwell, Ph.D., founded a leadership development institute in 1995 called INJOY. This institute is committed to increasing the effectiveness of people in all areas of life. Having studied his many books, Pastor Maxwell's writings and teachings focus on four primary areas that inspire **REAL** success:

Relationships

Equipping

Attitude

Leadership

One of the most inspirational lessons that I have learned from reading Pastor Maxwell's books is the principle of *"being a part of something greater than ourselves."* This principle simply means that in order to live a worthwhile, meaningful life, we must live a life that has not temporal but eternal impact. In order words, to become the person that God has created us to be—to reach our potential. *"You motivate me to dream big dreams and trust God for the impossible,*" is one of the best compliments that any of us can receive from a subordinate, peer, colleague, friend, family member, or an associate.[10]

In his book entitled, *The 108 Skills of Natural Born Leaders*, author Warren Blank defines 108 skills of successful leaders. He lists them into three categories and nine skill sets:

The Skills of Natural Born Leaders

Category	Skill Sets
Foundational skills	Expand self-awareness. Build rapport. Clarify expectations.
Leadership direction skills	Map the territory to identify the need to lead. Chart a course of leadership action. Develop others as leaders.
Leadership influence skills	Build the base to gain commitment. Influence others to willingly follow. Create a motivating environment.

Skills 61 and 63 are particularly insightful in that they articulate the leader's service to others. Skill 61, *Coach and Train*, are the one-to-one, face-to-face, day-to-day developmental activities. Coaching improves, extends, refines, or redirects behavior where a person already has some knowledge and skill. There are five successful coaching behaviors:

1. **Tell** people what they need to do to improve.

2. **Show** people how to improve.

3. **Clarify** the consequences of behavior.

4. **Provide** the big picture.

5. **Use** a confidence builder.

This involves good and on-going communication. Skill 63 is *Appraise Continuously*. Appraisal comes from the root word *praise*. Appraisal includes positive recognition and rewards for the full range of performance. The intent is to focus more on the person, not the specific project.

Concentrate on shaping employee's behavior, instead of grading people's behavior. Be a coach, not a judge or umpire. You personally may need to function more as a teacher, trainer or coach, and not just as a boss. Assist them in developing any new skills needed to perform competently. Call them by name, ask about their family, say thank you when they demonstrate the right attitude and effort.

Live a life filled with love, following the example of Christ. He loved us[a] and offered himself as a sacrifice for us, a pleasing aroma to God.

—Ephesians 5:2 NLT

---

[10] Maxwell, John C., *Developing the Leaders Around You*, Thomas Nelson Publishers, 1995, p. 189.

And walk in love, as Christ also hath loved us, and hath given himself for us an offering and a sacrifice to God for a sweet smelling savour.

—Ephesians 5:2 KJV

The Leadership Wisdom of Solomon: 28 Strategies for *Leading with Integrity*, by Pat Williams, senior vice president of the Orlando Magic NBA basketball team, is a book that reveals the wisdom of Solomon. Our world cries out for leaders with integrity. King Solomon transformed the tiny tribal nation of Israel into an economic and military superpower. His brilliance as an international financier made Israel the wealthiest nation of the ancient world. *And he did it with integrity.*

Solomon left us with twenty-eight profound leadership strategies—as valid today as when the proverbs were written. The same extraordinary wisdom that transformed Solomon's world can revolutionize every aspect of leadership—from assembling a cohesive team to managing a crisis—for any CEO, manager, pastor, coach, military strategist, or government leader. Four of the twenty-eight leadership strategies are worth highlighting.

The Leader's Moral Foundation (Proverbs 16:12)

The Ten Commandments form a basic moral code that will enable any leader to tell right from wrong in almost any situation. Some readers may not believe in God. But we cannot look at the source of Solomon's wisdom without clearly outlining this code as *his* code. Here are a few takeaways from Exodus 20:1–17 for moral leaders:

- *Moral leaders understand that God alone is God. He makes the rules and is worthy of respect.*
- *Moral leaders respect their follower's need for rest. It is immoral to exploit your people and work them to the point of exhaustion.*
- *Respect for others begins in the home. Respect is a basic moral requirement.*
- *Moral leaders not only refuse to commit murder but also refuse to harm other people in ways such as character assassination.*
- *Moral leaders deal honestly with employees and do not lie about competitors in order to gain some advantage.*

Quality and Excellence (Proverbs 20:8)

If you sell inferior products or services, you will lose your customers, your reputation, and your livelihood. Do not be too quick to undercut your competitor's prices; instead, deliver better quality and better service. People will notice, and your business will thrive. Let me suggest ten principles of quality and excellence that will set your organization apart.

- *Maintain a quality attitude.*
- *Build a quality team.*
- *Make every individual responsible for excellence.*

- *Inspire a passion for quality.*
- *Motivate your people to work hard.*
- *Welcome competition.*
- *Maintain consistency.*
- *Speed is a component of quality.*
- *Pay attention to detail.*
- *Make it fun!*

Doesn't God deserve your best effort?

The Spiritual Dimension of Leadership (Proverbs 21:1)

Solomon emphasizes the connection between faith and character. An effective leader exemplifies deeply ingrained traits of good character—things like:

- *Honesty*
- *Integrity*
- *Courage*
- *Diligence*
- *Dependability*
- *Fairness*
- *Compassion*
- *Generosity*
- *Humility*

These traits are built on a strong moral and ethical foundation.

The Breadth and Depth of a Great Leader (Proverbs 25:3)

An authentic leader is a lifelong learner. He can never afford to settle for the narrow and the shallow. Solomon said, "*Like the horizons for breadth and the ocean for depth, the understanding of a good leader is broad and deep*" (Proverbs 25:3, *MSG*). We must continually widen the breadth of our knowledge and deepen the oceans of our understanding.

A leader teaches, mentors, coaches, counsels, and empowers. Leaders inspire and influence others. They exemplify character. They are the living embodiment of the vision and values of the organization. Anyone with a loud voice can give orders, but it takes an authentic leader to impart knowledge and wisdom to his followers.

In order to teach, you must be intensely committed to continual learning. You must understand that learning is not a process the ended years ago when you graduated. Authentic leaders are committed to *lifelong learning*—and to *learning in depth*.

The breadth of a leader is his wide-ranging curiosity about a vast array of subjects and issues. The depth of a leader is his willingness to dig deeply into every issue, to master many fields of knowledge, to plumb the uttermost reaches of each subject.

The Seven Characteristics of Highly Successful Government Leaders

(From the blog of John Kamensky.) One former senior-level political appointee, Linda Springer, recently observed that a common set of successful characteristics of private sector leaders—being decisive, directive, and a risk taker—could actually undermine success in the public sector. So what works best in the public sector? Here are seven characteristics the most successful government leaders share:

Characteristic 1: Self-awareness.

Taking the Myers-Briggs personality test is only a start! The Emotional Intelligence Quotient, popularized by Daniel Goldman, and Marcus Buckingham's command to draw on your inner strengths, are also important ways to begin understanding yourself. One of the best pieces of advice I received was to never blame someone else, or the circumstances, for your failures, but rather to analyze what I did or didn't do to allow the failure to happen.

Characteristic 2: Authenticity.

Look at any leader you admire. One of the traits you'll likely see is their ability to empathize and connect with colleagues. Many of the most successful leaders share their personal vulnerabilities and lead with their heart as well as their head. Being passionate about your work and agency's mission can be part of this and is closely tied to the next three characteristics …

Characteristic 3: Reputation.

Would you follow someone you knew had little to no knowledge of your agency's mission or policy domain? This can often be the case when political appointees take charge of an agency. Having the right professional skills and credibility in the eyes of your peers, employees, and stakeholders is an important element for effective leadership. Yet, there are ways the uninitiated can succeed—just look at Charles Rossetti's leadership of the IRS in the 1990s. He was the first non-tax lawyer to head the agency and led a successful turnaround. But it's rare. Just look at the "heck of a job" done by past leaders of the Federal Emergency Management Agency and how their reputations colored their leadership …

Characteristic 4: Ethical behavior.

It's a question you wouldn't think you have to ask—but you do: Can your employees, and those for whom you work, trust you to do the right thing? The best leaders solicit feedback from those above and below them in the chain of command, always seeking to establish trust and, as a result, the ethical standards for individuals and the organization.

Characteristic 5: Willingness to listen.

Listening is a skill (a skill not easily mastered). It is more than just hearing someone else talk, it is a casting aside of the ego to allow oneself to sincerely care about what another has to say. Virtually all of the most senior leaders I've met are master listeners (and, by extension, learners). Fortunately for all you talkers, there are plenty of training resources on this topic.

Characteristic 6: Ability to communicate.

Creating effective ways to communicate your vision—directly, through incentives or through symbolic acts—can be one of the most powerful elements of getting action on key priorities. The Reinventing Government effort in the 1990s, led by Vice President Al Gore, relied not only on his speeches at events but also a set of principles. He got people to adopt these principles by sponsoring an award for teams of feds who lived up to these ideals. He called it the Hammer Award, named so to symbolize the breaking down of bureaucracy. It became a powerful symbol that communicated his vision to the front lines of government.

Characteristic 7: Optimism.

A "can do" positive outlook—even in the face of immense challenge—is often a defining characteristic of a good leader. I used to work at the Government Accountability Office, so I didn't come by this characteristic naturally. But with constant urging from a wonderful leader at the National Performance Review, Bob Stone, I learned the value and power of optimism. He was perennially optimistic about everything and seemed to be generally right. In fact, he called himself "energizer in chief," adopting the Energizer Bunny as his spirit animal. With this philosophy, things I thought were not possible actually happened, oftentimes because we started from the premise that they could!

Source: Kamensky, John, Government Executive e-blog, March 5, 2013.

One little act of kindness can have multiple results. To "walk in love" means that we continually do the little acts of kindness that can make life bearable and better for another person.

---

*The goal of life is to find out God's will
and to do it.*

NOTES:

_____

_____

_____

_____

Powerful Influence:
Your Life Either Sheds Light or Casts a Shadow

The way we live does affect others for good or for bad. This is a sobering and challenging truth that should influence the way we as Christians walk and talk. It's surprising how many people go through life without ever recognizing that their feelings

toward other people are largely determined by their feeling toward themselves, and if
you're not comfortable within yourself, you can't be comfortable with others.

—Sidney Harris

In her first twelve months in office, Indonesia's Megawati Sukarnoputri has brought two rare qualities to the presidential palace: *peace and quiet*. What a transition from the former leadership. Mrs. Sukarnoputri has said little in public since her election in July 2001, avoiding the outbursts of her predecessor, the blind cleric Abdurrahman Wahid, who often sent the country's currency markets into turmoil. The equity markets seem to be thanking her. Indonesia is the world's fourth most populous country, but has a relatively small stock exchange, with a capitalization of just $36 billion. The sense of relative calm in Jakarta has helped to reassure consumers and share prices have risen as demand has fueled economic growth. Private consumption rose 9.2 percent in real terms during the second half of 2001.[11]

The largest gathering of world leaders—more than 150—in history took place on Wednesday, September 5, 2002, to chart the course of the United Nations in the twenty-first century—particularly its efforts to forge peace. It opened with a call for peace and an end to war. As the meeting began, it was clouded by the killings of three United Nations workers in West Timor. Former U.S. President William J. Clinton stated that he was "deeply saddened" to learn of the three murders and that the United Nations must be prepared to confront such hostilities. He specifically called on the Indonesian authorities "to put a stop to these abuses," as former President Abdurrahman Wahid was in the audience. At the urging of United Nations Secretary General Kofi Annan, the leaders held a minute of silence at the start of the meeting to commemorate the deaths of the three aid workers slain after an angry Indonesian mob and militiamen attacked and burned the office of the United Nations High Commissioner for Refugees.

In an article entitled, *"World Leaders meet for Millennium Summit,"* at the conclusion of the summit, world leaders were expected to adopt a so-called Millennium Declaration, which commits to eradicate poverty, promote education, and reverse the spread of HIV/AIDS. Noting that more than five million people have lost their lives in wars during the past decade, the document says, "we will spare no effort to free our peoples from the scourge of war." The nine-page draft vows to promote democracy and strengthen respect for human rights and fundamental freedoms, including "the right to development"—a key demand by Third World countries (*USATODAY.com*, September 5, 2000).

In whom the god of this world hath blinded the minds of them which believe not, lest the
light of the glorious gospel of Christ, who is the image of God, should shine unto them.
For we preach not ourselves, but Christ Jesus the Lord, and ourselves your servants for
Jesus' sake. For God, who commanded the light to shine out of darkness, hath shined in
our hearts, to give the light of the knowledge of the glory of God in the face of Jesus
Christ. But we have this treasure in earthen vessels, that the excellency of the power may
be of God, and not of us.

—2 Corinthians 4:4–7 KJV

---

[11] *Financial Times* newspaper, "Indonesian thrives on Peace and Quiet," July 8, 2002, by Tom McCawley, p. 17.

For the god of this world has blinded the unbelievers' minds [that they should not discern the truth], preventing them from seeing the illuminating light of the Gospel of the glory of Christ (the Messiah), Who is the Image and Likeness of God. For what we preach is not ourselves but Jesus Christ as Lord, and ourselves [merely] as your servants (slaves) for Jesus' sake. For God Who said, Let light shine out of darkness, has shone in our hearts so as [to beam forth] the Light for the illumination of the knowledge of the majesty and glory of God [as it is manifest in the Person and is revealed] in the face of Jesus Christ (the Messiah). However, we possess this precious treasure [the divine Light of the Gospel] in [frail, human] vessels of earth, that the grandeur and exceeding greatness of the power may be shown to be from God and not from ourselves.

—2 Corinthians 4:4–7 AMP

We **cannot** *hide the gospel*

*That ye may be blameless and harmless, the sons of God, without rebuke, in the midst of a crooked and preserve nation, among whom ye shine as **lights** in the world*

—Philippians 2:15 KJV

So that no one can criticize you. Live clean, innocent lives as children of God, shining like bright lights in a world full of crooked and perverse people.

—Philippians 2:15 NLT

Great men are little men expanded. Great lives are ordinary lives intensified. The Apostle Paul gives us a natural example of advancing through adversity. Because Paul was forced to spend all but seven years of his ministry in prison, we get to read his life-changing epistles, two thousand years later. A man gifted with compassion and encouragement, he authored thirteen New Testament books of *The Holy Bible* with impactful messages:

Letters to the churches:

Romans—Considered Paul's greatest work, he explores the significance of Jesus' sacrificial death. Behavior must be built upon belief. It does not determine the blessing. Instead, the blessing should determine the behavior.

1 Corinthians—Application of Christian principles to carnality in the individual and in the church. Corinth was a hub of commerce, degraded culture, and idolatrous religion.

2 Corinthians—Paul defends his apostolic credentials and authority. Most have repented and some have not.

Galatians—The *Christian's "Declaration of Independence*," blessing comes from God on the basis of faith, not law.

Ephesians—Addressed to a group of believers who are rich beyond measure in Jesus, yet living as beggars. "In Christ" appears about thirty-five times, more than any other New Testament book.

Philippians—Only in Christ are real unity and joy possible. Paul writes a thank-you note to the believers at Philippi for their help in his hour of need.

Colossians—Perhaps the most Christ-centered book in the Bible. Focuses on the Head (Christ). Its purpose is to show that Christ is preeminent.

1 Thessalonians—Christ is seen as the believer's hope of salvation, now and at His coming. Steadfastness in the Lord is key.

2 Thessalonians—Paul deals with a misunderstanding spawned by false teachers regarding the coming day of the Lord. The major concept is the return of Christ (mentioned 318 times in the New Testament).

Letters to individuals:

1 Timothy—Paul warns young Timothy to be a guard to avoid false teachers and greedy motives. Timothy was to organize and oversee the Asian churches as a faithful minister of God. By now, Christianity was illegal.

2 Timothy—Writing from Roman prison, Paul writes a letter of encouragement.

Titus—Titus served as Paul's special apostolic delegate to Corinth. Paul traveled with Timothy and Titus. He left Timothy in Ephesus and traveled on to Crete with Titus. He left Titus in Crete to provide leadership for the church there. In this short epistle to Titus, Paul wrote directions similar to those he had written in his first letter to Timothy. The difference is one of emphasis. In First Timothy, Paul's emphasis is on the leadership of the local church. In Titus, the emphasis is on the organization of the local church.

Philemon—In this one page book, Paul writes a postcard about a master-slave relationship. Philemon forgives his runaway slave Onesimus for running away, after he receives Christ.

Encourage and inspire someone today. Help them to reach their potential through your zeal, passion, and love of life! Be the leader that God has called you to be and *serve* someone through your gift as God has preordained before the foundation of the world. Share God's plan to prosper them through the plan that He has for their life (Jeremiah 29:11).

NOTES:

_____

_____

_____

_____

Questions for Personal Reflection or Group Discussion

1. How do you let your light shine at work?

   _____

   _____

   _____

2. Which of the Seven characteristics of Highly Successful Leaders applies to you?

   _____

   _____

   _____

3. What makes you a good leader?

   _____

   _____

   _____

4. Give two examples of how you lead God's way.

   _____

   _____

   _____

5. Which leadership strategy best fits your purpose as a leader in the workplace?

   _____

   _____

   _____

ON LEADERSHIP

A leader is one who knows the way, goes the way, and shows the way.

The ten 'Sacred Bulls' that create obstacles to your progress at work are the Bulls of:

1. Denial: *I don't see the problem, so it isn't there.*

2. Blind spots and Shortcuts: *What I don't like can't be important.*

3. Self-Interest: *Always look out for number one.*

4. Mind Reading: *People should know what I want without being told.*

5. Blame: *If something goes wrong, it has to be somebody's fault.*

6. Being Nice: *Avoid conflict at all times.*

7. Perfection: *If it's not perfect, it's nothing.*

8. Fairness: *I don't need to negotiate for what I want; I just want fairness.*

9. Excuses: *There's always a good reason why I don't follow the rules everyone else works by.*

10. Being Right: *There's a right way and a wrong way; my way is right.*

Chief Executive Officer

Politician

News Reporter/Anchor

Government Official

Vice President, Finance

Pastor

Administrator

Doctor

Chef

Architect

Director

Head Coach

PART THREE

The Mentoring Years ...

Raising the level of productivity of others

*Here's another way to put it: You're here to be **light**, bringing out the God-colors in the world. God is not a secret to be kept. We're going public with this, as public as a city on a hill. If I make you light-bearers, you don't think I'm going to hide you under a bucket, do you? I'm putting you on a light stand. Now that I've put you there on a hilltop, on a light stand—shine! Keep open house; be generous with your lives. By opening up to others, you'll prompt people to open up with God, this generous Father in heaven.*

—Matthew 5:14–16 AMP

*Let your **light** so shine before men, that they may see your good works, and glorify your Father which is in heaven.*

—Matthew 5:16 KJV

*A*s mentors, we have a responsibility to raise the level of productivity of others that are within our sphere of influence—through *excellence*. Beginning with self, we must have determination and zeal to see others excel and to become what God has called them to be. In Genesis, chapter one, verse 28, God gives four specific instructions after creating man in His image and in His likeness: *"Be fruitful, and multiply, and replenish the earth, and subdue it."* "Multiply" means to raise the level of productivity of others.

Likewise, Jesus taught a multitude of followers and His disciples, during His first public sermon—Sermon on the Mount—*"Let your light so shine before men, that they may see your good works, and glorify your Father which is in heaven* (Matthew 5:16)." Our *light* exposes sin, extends brightness, projects, shines, radiates, and illuminates. Why this teaching and why at this time during His public ministry? It was time for Jesus to teach throughout all of Galilee, preach the gospel of the kingdom, and heal all manner of sickness and disease among the people (Matthew 4:23). It was vital at this time in history that men see His *good works* so that God be glorified in heaven.

First, be an inspiration—something that people can see and aspire to become. The life of Dr. Martin Luther King, Jr., is a true inspiration to millions. Secondly, walk by faith and not by sight (2 Corinthians 5:7). Trust in God and not the circumstances or situations at work. Change is a constant and consistent reality in this world, but God never changes. Thirdly, be a great communicator and explain what you mean. Effective communication does not take place until the recipient of your message hears, receives, and acknowledges the message. A confirmation of understanding is necessary. Poor communication is perhaps the biggest challenge facing the workplace today, especially in corporate America. There is too much emphasis on achieving results—whether clearly understood or not—with little or no direction, guidance, nor proper roadmap to assist in delivering the expected outcome or results. Misconceptions, misinterpretations, and misunderstandings are the direct result of poor communication. Evangelist Billy Graham is a great communicator as evidenced by the thousands, perhaps millions, of people that have confessed Jesus Christ as their personal Lord and Saviour over the fifty years that he has preached the gospel. Crusade after crusade, he effectively communicates the comforting message that *"God loves you and He gave His only begotten Son for you. Come to Jesus …"*

Chapter Seven

Be an Inspiration,
Not an Obstacle

"I have an inner urge calling me to serve humanity."

—Reverend Dr. Martin Luther King, Jr.
remarks prior to this ordination
as a minister at the age of nineteen.

*This then is the message which we have heard of him, and declare unto you, that God is **light**, and in him is no darkness at all. If we say that we have fellowship with him, and walk in darkness, we lie, and do not the truth: but if we walk in the **light**, as he is in the **light**, we have fellowship one with another, and the blood of Jesus Christ his Son cleanseth us from all sin.*

—1 John 1:5–7 KJV

This, in essence, is the message we heard from Christ and are passing on to you: God is light, pure light; there's not a trace of darkness in him. If we claim that we experience a shared life with him and continue to stumble around in the dark, we're obviously lying through our teeth—we're not living what we claim. But if we walk in the light, God himself being the light, we also experience a shared life with one another, as the sacrificed blood of Jesus, God's Son, purges all our sin.

—1 John 1:5–7 MSG

Inspire others to excel through your character, work ethic, and integrity.

*I*n the book of Genesis, chapter one, God reveals unto Adam that he is blessed and to be fruitful, multiply, replenish the earth, and subdue it. God's specific instructions are to be *productive, raise the level of productivity of those around us, leave a deposit in the earth for the next generation,* and *to control our environment.* What an awesome responsibility that God entrusts us with! It takes inspiration to be a productive person and to raise the level of productivity of others because our actions inspire them to do so.

Reverend Dr. Martin Luther King, Jr. is one of the world's greatest inspirations. He truly inspired all Americans to change an entire culture, custom, practice, and mindset—discrimination based upon skin color. Dr. King is the only American-born citizen who has a birthday as a holiday in his name. He defined greatness through the service that he tirelessly rendered. From 1955 to 1968, he led peaceful demonstrations against evil throughout the United States, particularly in the south. He inspired millions to follow his peaceful demonstrations. This was partly because of his stance on not being afraid to die for a cause that is just, right, fair, equitable, and scriptural. Tapped as one of the most important speeches in the twentieth century, Dr. King's *I Have A Dream* is replayed every year as America celebrates the life and legacy of this great servant of the Lord on January fifteenth.

Having skipped two grades in high school, Dr. King began college at the tender age of fifteen. He was such an inspirational leader that he led a 381-day bus boycott in Montgomery, Alabama in response to Rosa Parks' refusal to needlessly abandon her seat. During the 1950s, the state law stipulated that she had to surrender her seat to a white person, even if others seats were available. This law made no sense, but the courage to challenge this was lacking. God is no respecter of persons (James 2:9), and finally, under leadership, the state of Alabama's decision to arbitrarily defy God's Word was ignored. Dr. King declared that *"It is better to walk in humility than to ride in humiliation."* It was a spark that caught thousands on fire to take an active role in bankrupting a corrupt state government system. However, his compassion was equally comforting when he said that through nonviolent and peaceful protests, *"We can turn any man into a friend."*

Dr. King was so focused on his calling to be an inspirational leader that he only granted one television interview. This was granted to Arnold McCalah. Yet, he was arrested thirty times for taking a stand for justice, righteousness, equity, and fair treatment for all people. On the eve of his assassination, April 3, 1968, Dr. King delivered his infamous *I've Been to the Mountaintop* speech. It was a night in which he was sick and had sent Dr. Ralph Abernathy to speak in his absence. Instead, he arrived and delivered a powerful and inspirational address that is replayed every year for us to remember. He described his mountaintop experience as if he knew that April 4, 1968, would be his last day as an earthen vessel for the Lord. Most notably, at Dr. King's home going service, one of his sermons was played and he specifically requested that no one boast about his life. Instead, he requested that we remember him in the following way:

- He tried to give his life serving others.
- He tried to love somebody.
- Remember him a drum major for justice.
- Don't mention his awards or his Nobel Peace Prize.

Forty-five years after his assassination, he remains a model for all pastors. His impact on the church, particularly the African-American church, and the community it serves remains the standard against which all preachers are measured. The chronology of Dr. King's life is long and impressive, but several key accomplishments that changed America during his lifetime are worth noting:

1947 Licensed to preach and begins assisting his father, who is Pastor of Ebenezer Baptist Church in Atlanta.

1951 Graduates from Crozer with Bachelor of Divinity Degree. He is the class valedictorian and winner of the Pearl Plafker Award for most outstanding student. He begins doctoral studies in theology at Boston University.

1956 June 4: U.S. District court rules racial segregation on Alabama's city bus lines is unconstitutional.

1957 September 9: Congress passes the 1957 Civil Rights Act, *first civil rights legislation since Reconstruction.*

1959 February: Dr. and Mrs. King travel to India as guests of Prime Minister Nehru to study Gandhi's techniques of nonviolence.

1960 May 6: The 1960 Civil Rights Act is signed.

December: U.S. Supreme Court declares discrimination in bus terminal restaurants operated for the service of interstate passengers is a violation of the Interstate Commerce Act.

1961 November: Interstate Commerce Commission bans segregation on buses, trains, and supportive facilities.

1964 January 3: Time magazine names Dr. King *Man of the Year.*

1964 July 2: Witnesses the signing of the 1964 Civil Rights Act by President Lyndon Johnson—*the most far-reaching civil rights legislation since Reconstruction.*

1964 December 10: Awarded the Nobel Peace Prize in Oslo, Norway—the youngest person to win the prize.

1965 August 6: President Johnson signs the 1965 Voting Rights Act.

1967 November 7: Carl Stokes elected mayor of Cleveland, Ohio—the first black elected mayor of a major U.S. city.

1968 April 7: The President declares a national day of mourning for King.

1986 First National King Holiday celebrated.

"Our lives begin to end the day we become silent about things that matter."

—Dr. Martin Luther King, Jr.

"Let freedom ring ... " are the concluding words from perhaps the most memorable speech in the history of the United States of America: *"Let freedom ring from the mighty mountains of New York ... the heightening Alleghenies of Pennsylvania ... the snowcapped Rockies of Colorado ... the curvaceous slopes of California ... But not only that ... from Stone Mountain of Georgia ... from Lookout Mountain*

of Tennessee ... from every hill and molehill of Mississippi ... from every mountainside, let freedom ring."

Source: *I Have a Dream*, Martin Luther King, Jr., pages 29–31, 1993, Anniversary Edition.

"New issues have emerged as a result of rapid technological development, such as the fight to preserve the environment, and a woman's right to reproductive choice. These are being addressed all over the U.S. by non-violent protest, inspired by Dr. King's message. It is my conviction that as new technologies emerge, they often bring tradition into conflict with new values. The tools which Dr. King has given us will enable us to confront each new issue as it arises. The struggles may change, but the tools remain constant, and for that we are indebted."

Source: "A Remembrance of Dr. Martin Luther King, Jr.," Benedict J. Fernandez—www.kodak.com, January 15, 2001.

The Power of Frequent Career-Building Power Chats

At many federal agencies, career development comes up in one of two situations:

- When it is performance review time, or
- When an employee announces plans to leave.

With only a few minutes of conversation a day, managers can dramatically improve employee engagement, retention, and results. Career development tends to center on forms, checklists, and annual processes. Feedback that should take place daily is compressed into one long annual meeting where nervous employees are told where they have fallen short, and they in turn promise to remedy shortcomings in the year to come.

Iterative conversations let employees slow down enough to reflect, develop, and verbalize deep insights and to consider how to leverage their growing capacity. There are three distinct types of conversations that are important to keep employees happy:

Hindsight conversations are meant to help employees look backward and inward to reflect on who they are, where they have been, what they love, and where they excel. This kind of conversation requires employees to be self-aware and deeply engaged, but managers can facilitate by providing thoughtful feedback.

Foresight conversations should guide employees to look outward toward the changes and trends they want to see in the bigger picture of their careers. These conversations should help employees apply what they have learned about themselves through hindsight conversations and put that in context of what is going on around them.

Insight conversations bring together the fruits of hindsight and foresight. They involve employees and managers working together to determine future actions to achieve career objectives, with managers guiding employees into practical steps toward their goals. Managers should help employees learn to grow in place, replacing "onward and upward" with "forward and forward." The challenge is for managers to broaden career conversations beyond just jobs, promotions, and raises, and to focus on what employees need to experience, know, learn, and be able to do.

Source: Jochum, Elizabeth Newell, *Government Executive*, Management Matters, November 14, 2012.

_____

_____

_____

_____

"Inspiration" Defined

Inspiration, in its original Greek language, is translated as *theopneustos* and means "inspired by God." It comes from two words—*Theos* (God) and *Pneō* (to breathe). The scripture that best describes this word is found in 2 Timothy 3:16:

> *All scripture is given by inspiration of God, and is profitable for doctrine, for reproof, for correction, for instruction in righteousness.*

> —2 Timothy 3:16 KJV

> *Every Scripture is God-breathed (given by His inspiration) and profitable for instruction, for reproof and conviction of sin, for correction of error and discipline in obedience, [and] for training in righteousness (in holy living, in conformity to God's will in thought, purpose, and action).*

> —2 Timothy 3:16 AMP

Inspiration of God describes the unique character of scripture:
- It is not only written by men, but authored by God
- For doctrine means to tell one what to believe
- For reproof means to tell one what is wrong.
- For correction means to tell one how to correct wrong.
- For instruction in righteousness means to tell one how to live.

Why?

> *By using scripture, a man of God can be completely prepared to do every good thing.*

> —2 Timothy 3:17 NIRV

> *That the man of God may be perfect, thoroughly furnished unto all good works.*

> —2 Timothy 3:17 KJV

Perfect (proficient or capable) is having everything needed to do what God wants. Thoroughly furnished means equipped. God's inspired Word, properly used and applied, provides all that we need for life and ministry.

Everywhere I go I find that people—both leaders and individuals—are asking one basic question: 'Is there any hope for the future? Is there any hope for peace, justice, and prosperity in our generation?

—Billy Graham

*"If you have a job without aggravations,
you don't have a job."*
—MALCOMB FORBES

Any Definition of a Successful Life Must Include Serving Others

Serve Man

There are high spots in all of our lives, and most of them have come about through encouragement from someone else. I don't care how great, how famous, or successful a man or woman may be, each hungers for applause.

—George Adams

The deepest principle in human nature is the craving to be appreciated.

But he that is greatest among you shall be your servant.

—Matthew 23:11 KJV

Whoever is your servant is the greatest among you.

—Matthew 23:11 NCV

As Jesus denounces the customs, practices, philosophies, hypocrisies, and traditions of the Pharisees and the scribes, He teaches us that to be a servant means to be a "minister" or "attendant." That is the true meaning of the word.

We all start out in *dependent* relationships. Dependent means:

- Needing and relying on others for life needs
- Being unable or unwilling to provide for one's self
- Relying on the aid of another for support

Some become *independent*:

- Not needing or relying on others for life or relational needs

- Being able to provide for one's self
- Free from the influence, guidance, and control of others

God call us to be *interdependent* and have interdependent relationships. Interdependent means:

- Committing who we are and what we have to serve others
- Knowing what we can offer to, and when we need from, others
- Enjoying the fruit of diverse gifts operating in unison ("mutually dependent")

Interdependent relationships reflect God's design for the church. When we all do what we were created to do … and we do it together … we will be a healthy, interdependent, and harmonious church.

<u>Source</u>: Bugbee and Cousins, 2005.

We are to serve others with the gift that God has freely given to us. The word "gift" is defined as *"Dōrea"* in the New Testament and denotes a "free gift," stressing its gratuitous character. It is always used in the New Testament of a spiritual or supernatural gift. Examples include John 4:10, Acts 8:20 and 11:17, Romans 5:15, 2 Corinthians 9:15, Ephesians 3:7, and Hebrews 6:4. In Ephesians 4:7, *"according to the measure of the gift of Christ,"* the "gift" is that given by Christ. In Acts 2:28, *"the gift of the Holy Ghost,"* the "gift" being the Holy Ghost himself.

This free gift is never taken away by God. It is either used or remains dormant as it relates to glorifying God. According to His Word, we are responsible and accountable for our gifts and to fulfill our purpose for being birthed into the earth—*"For the gifts and calling of God are without repentance"* (Romans 11:29).

Through the will (choice) of man, Romans 12:6–8 identifies the seven functional gifts. Functional gifts specifically identify our responsibilities toward society and one another in the body of Christ. How we conduct our everyday affairs in the presence of people who have no relationship with God (verse 20), as well as the brothers and sisters in Christ (verse 13), is taught in this scripture. The *functional* gifts are:

- *Prophesy* (encouragement by the measure of faith),
- *Ministry* (service with patience),
- *Exhortation* (wise counsel),
- *Teaching* (instruction),
- *Giving* (giving without complicating matters—simplicity is key),
- *Ruling* (diligent leadership), and
- *Showing mercy* (cheerful compassion).

Gift (*Hebrew or Greek word*)—Original meaning in Hebrew or Greek

Prophesy *(proph•teia)*—speaking forth the mind and counsel of God. The declaration of that which cannot be known by natural means (the foretelling of the will of God whether with reference to past, present, or future).

Ministry *(diakonia)*—service; servant of the Lord in preaching and teaching.

Exhortation *(paraklēsis)*—a calling to one's side; to one's aid; consolation and comfort.

Teaching (*didaskalia*)—that which is taught; doctrine; instruction; learning. Occurs fifteen times in the New Testament.

Giving (*charizomai*)—"to show favor or kindness"; to give freely, bestow graciously. Refers mostly to what is "given" by God.

Ruling (*proistēmi*)—to stand before, to lead, attend to (indicating care and diligence). Is translated "to rule" (middle voice), with reference to a local church.

Showing mercy (*eleos*)—the outward manifestation of pity.

Upon further examination of the twelfth chapter of Romans, the Apostle Paul instructs us on proper responsibilities toward the society in general. Beginning in verse 3, he reminds us that through the grace that has been given by God, we are to be humble and not to think too highly of ourselves. This is applicable to all situations and circumstances in life. As God has dealt to all men, and women, the measure of faith, we are commanded to exercise our gift(s) with humility and in faith. Paul's purpose for this instruction is so that we would be mindful that each of the seven functional spiritual gifts have a different benefit within the body of Christ, yet we are one body in Christ and each of us are members one of another (verses 4–6).

As we *function together* as one in love, which is the overriding theme, it becomes less challenging to apply God's Word to our daily lives. In verses 9–21, we are specifically instructed to love, serve, extend kindness, be instant in prayer, be honest, serve the Lord, overcome evil with good, live peaceably with all men, and not seek revenge. These instructions apply to all situations and to all of God's people. The blessings of God's functional gifts allow us to remain in obedience to His Word. Circumstances and situations shall not prevail, but the Word of God shall prevail in our life!

If a man's gift is encouraging, let him encourage. If a man's gift is ministry, let him serve with patience. If a man's gift is ruling, let him do so through diligent leadership. If a man's gift is teaching, let him instruct. If a man's gift is exhortation, let him do so through wise counsel. If a man loves to give, let him give without complicating matters. If a man's gift is showing mercy, let him be cheerful in doing so.

> *We have different gifts, according to the grace given to each of us. If your gift is prophesying, then prophesy in accordance with your[a] faith;*

—Romans 12:6 NIV

> *Having then gifts differing according to the grace that is given to us ...*

—Romans 12:6 KJV

Serve God

To *glorify* means to praise and worship (Psalm 86:9). It means to admire, point out the good in, and recognize as glorious. A Christian's greatest calling is to glorify God through his or her actions, words, and character (Matthew 5:16). Christians glorify God by obeying Him and living His way.

Specific examples include sexual purity (1 Corinthians 6:20), choosing the right words (1Peter 4:11), living as a Christian (Romans 15:6), and imitating Jesus (John 17:10–11). As Christians, we are followers of Jesus Christ (Acts 11:26 and 26:28; 1 Peter 4:16). We belong to Christ. Christians commit themselves to Christ and become increasingly like Him. We trust Jesus Christ to guide our decisions, actions, and attitudes. To handle yourself, use your *head*. To handle others, use your *heart*.

This then is the message which we have heard of him, and declare unto you, that God is light, and in him is no darkness at all. If we say that we have fellowship with him, and walk in darkness, we lie, and do not the truth: But if we walk in the light, as he is in the light, we have fellowship one with another, and the blood of Jesus Christ his Son cleanseth us from all sin.

—1 John 1:5–7 KJV

This is the message we heard from Jesus[a] and now declare to you: God is light, and there is no darkness in him at all. [6] So we are lying if we say we have fellowship with God but go on living in spiritual darkness; we are not practicing the truth. But if we are living in the light, as God is in the light, then we have fellowship with each other, and the blood of Jesus, his Son, cleanses us from all sin.

—1 John 1:5–7 NLT

God is perfect and good. There is no sin or evil in Him. This has implications for followers of Him as we look to Him as our Heavenly Father. (1) Walk in darkness means to walk in sin. If we walk in darkness, we cannot enjoy a close relationship with God. (2) To walk in His light, which means to live free from the bondage of sin, makes true communion between believers possible. (3) The blood of Jesus represents the cleansing and ultimate defense against sin's presence and power.

As they were walking along and talking together, suddenly a chariot of fire and horses of fire appeared and separated the two of them, and Elijah went up to heaven in a whirlwind.

—2 Kings 2:11 NIV

And it came to pass, as they still went on, and talked, that, behold, there appeared a chariot of fire, and horses of fire, and parted them both asunder; and Elijah went up by a whirlwind into heaven.

—2 Kings 2:11 KJV

Elijah followed Enoch in being taken into heaven without dying. This parallels Genesis 5:24—*"And Enoch walked with God: and he was not; for God took him."*

Elijah was a well-loved prophet of Israel who took a stand for God against false religious leaders and kings (1 Kings 17:1; 18; 21:17–29). He is best known for discrediting Baal and Baal's prophets on

Mount Carmel and for hearing a still small voice (1Kings 18; 19:12–13). Rather than dying, Elijah was taken up into heaven in a whirlwind. John the Baptist was sometimes referred to as Elijah. Elijah appeared to Jesus on the mount of transfiguration. His name means *Yahweh is God.* He was succeeded by Elisha.

NOTES:

_____

_____

_____

_____

Be Prepared to Inspire!

During your lifetime, you will directly or indirectly influence the lives of ten thousand other people. How will you influence them?

Demetrius, for example, is well spoken of by everyone and even by the truth itself. He was a Christian commended for his witness. *"Demetrius hath good report of all men, and of the truth itself: yea, and we also bear record; and ye know that our record is true"* (3 John 12).

Prepare for the day that your mentor will not be around (Joshua-Moses; Paul-Timothy; Elijah-Elisha; David-Solomon). God is always preparing someone to carrying out His work and to take it to the next level. Do not allow someone that you can influence to be untrained or unlearned as they progress to the next level. Do not leave them evading questions, getting caught in scams, orchestrating unscrupulous business practices, or participating in unrighteousness. Make a difference in the life of another person and do it now!

Inspire in the midst of the distractions

Several polls indicate that there are five primary office distractions. They are:

1. Chatting

2. Personal phone calls

3. Electronic noises (computer, cell phones, pagers)

4. Air quality

5. Lighting

Source: American Society of Interior Designers; Stephen Viscusi, author of "On the Job—How to Make It in the Real World of Work."

In the midst of these top five office distractions, there are six primary types of disruptive workers to contend with at the office. Disruptive co-workers fall into the following categories with a brief description of each:

- *The Chatterbox*—Talkative, ignorant, selfish, irritating, unaware of others, disrespectful, uncommunicative, and boring. They are talkaholics.
- *The Competitor*—Provocative, fearless, paranoid, offensive, pushy, aggressive, resentful, confrontational, and sabotaging. Always looking for a fight.
- *The Gossip*—Indiscreet, insecure, fault-finding, competitive, hurtful, self-righteous, offensive, and angry.
- *The Jokester*—Annoying, insecure, weak, obnoxious, selfish, corny, offensive, superficial, desperate for attention, and unaware of others.
- *The Cut-You Downer*—Arrogant, mean, belittling, hateful, self-righteous, condescending, threatening, insecure, underhanded, and fault-finding.
- *The Gloom and Doom Victim*—Masochistic, guilt-ridden, worrisome, sabotaging, resentful, rigid, selfish, sad, negative, petty, lackadaisical, and defensive.

Source: Irizarry, Lisa, "How to Handle Disruptive Co-Workers," *The Star-Ledger*, May 26, 2002, p. 2, Section Two.

How to Deal with Difficult People

We all have to deal with difficult people from time to time. Below are some tips to help you to manage these relationships:

- Be a forgiver. This does not mean putting up with abuse. It does mean to remember Jesus' advice to His soon-to-be-persecuted disciples: Turn the other cheek (Matthew 5:38–42), and forgive abundantly (Matthew 18:21–22).
- Study what the Bible says about dealing with people:
  - *A soft answer turns away wrath, but a harsh word stirs up anger* (Proverbs 15:1)
  - *Behold, how good and pleasant it is for brethren to dwell together in unity!* (Psalm 133:1)
- Learn from diplomatic friends. Choose your words carefully. Non-confrontational tones go a long way with multiple audiences.
- Make a list of the difficult person's positive qualities and look for ways to genuinely express your appreciation for them.
- Remember, Jesus loves this person too. And because of His love, He died for that person just as much as for you and me. So always bathe your antagonist in lots of prayer. You might be surprised—as I've been—at the wonders prayers can work.

Source: Schurch, Maylan, *Signs of the Times*, January 2013.

Let us live that when we die, even the undertaker will be sorry. You can preach a better sermon with your life than with your lips. As God gave us His Word through inspiration, inspire others, despite their faults, through the Word of God. Lead by example. Inspire others to excel through your character, work ethic, and integrity. Be an inspiration, not an obstacle.

Questions for Personal Reflection or Group Discussion

1. Being an inspiration to others requires how much effort on your part? Please explain.

   _____

   _____

   _____

2. Dr. King and Evangelist Graham were an inspiration to millions. Name a few inspirational persons who motivated you toward greatness.

   _____

   _____

   _____

3. Describe Matthew 23:11 in your own words.

   _____

   _____

   _____

4. Name your spiritual gift(s). How are you using it/them to make this world a better place?

   _____

   _____

   _____

5. As it relates to difficult people, how do you propose to handle this situation?

   _____

   _____

   _____

food for thought

ON AVOIDING OBSTACLES

Following the path of least resistance is what makes rivers—and people—crooked.

Chapter Eight

Walk by Faith, Not by Sight

"For we walk by faith, not by sight!"

> —*Dr. Frederick K.C. Price*, Pastor, Crenshaw Christian Center,
> Los Angeles, California, as he concludes his weekly sermons
> through the Ever Increasing Faith Ministries
> broadcast on over 115 television stations worldwide.

For we walk by faith, not by sight.

—2 Corinthians 5:7 KJV

For we walk by faith [we [a] regulate our lives and conduct ourselves by our conviction or belief respecting man's relationship to God and divine things, with trust and holy fervor; thus we walk] not by sight or appearance.

—2 Corinthians 5:7 AMP

Despite constant change, obstacles, and disappointments, walk by faith.

*H*ow you think about a problem is more important than the problem itself. So always think positively. We are made up of three parts—*soul* (our will, thoughts, and emotions), *body* (our means of survival on earth through the five sensory perceptions—taste, smell, sight, touch, and hearing), and *spirit* (the "real" you—how we make contact with God Almighty). The inner man, *spirit*, is made alive when we confess Jesus Christ as our personal Lord and Saviour—the prayer of salvation. We then enter into *THE* faith of Jesus, who is the author and finisher of *our* faith (Hebrews 12:2). As an heir to the inheritance of our Heavenly Father, and co-heir with Jesus Christ, we can and should walk by faith and not by sight.

We are bombarded daily by visual stimulation—things that we *see*—that influence our actions, thoughts, and words. We are, however, on an assignment in the earth, as ambassadors for Christ, to fulfill God's plan for our lives. Better yet, we already have the victory through God's Word.

But thanks be to God, which giveth us the victory through our Lord Jesus Christ.

—1 Corinthians 15:57 KJV

But we thank God! He gives us the victory through our Lord Jesus Christ.

—1 Corinthians 15:57 NCV

"I don't know the key to success, but the key to failure is trying to please everybody."
—BILL COSBY

When Dave Thomas died in early 2002, he left behind more than just thousands of Wendy's Restaurants. He also left a legacy of being a practical, hard-working man who was respected for his down-to-earth values.

Among the pieces of good advice that have outlived the smiling entrepreneur is his view of what Christians should be doing with their lives. In his book entitled, *Well Done*, Thomas said, "Roll-up-your-shirtsleeve Christians see Christianity as faith and action. They still make the time to talk with God through prayer, study scripture with devotion, be super-active in their church, and take their ministry to others to spread the Good Word." He went on to say they are "anonymous people who may be doing even more good than all the well-known Christians in the world."

But someone will say, "You have faith. I do good works." Show me your faith that doesn't do good works. And I will show you my faith by what I do.

—James 2:18 NIRV

A living faith is a working faith.

Management Style Fads Come and Go

Over the past century, businesses have embraced many different management strategies. Some have been inspired by science more than by art. Today's workplace is a mosaic of them:

1908   Model Ts begin assembly line. Henry Ford's scientific method revolutionizes the manufacturing process.

1923   Alfred Sloan takes the helm at General Motors. His genius for marketing and organization at the company pushes him to the forefront of leading management practices.

1956   William Whyte's book *The Organization Man* criticizes the sterile bureaucracy of American business and calls for immediate change.

1960   *The Human Side of Enterprise* by Douglas McGregor introduces a new concept: Business with a human face. Employees and customers benefit.

1963   Boston Consulting Group is founded, beginning the rise and influence of professional management consultants.

1982   *In Search of Excellence*, by two McKinsey consultants, touches off a craze of management books and fads that American firms glom onto in search of answers. *The One Minute Manager* becomes a big seller.

1993   Business process re-engineering emerges during lean times. This translates into mass layoffs at many companies.

1995   The Internet era begins. Information workers emerge as do stock options, lattes, and office toys galore! This nonsense does not last long.

2003   AOL Time Warner embraces a low-key chief executive officer and a back-to-basics approach.

I will take God's Word over any and all of man's management fads any day. In the introduction of this book, I demonstrated through God's Word that he does not change. There is tremendous comfort in knowing that we serve a God that cannot, and will not, change. His Word is His bond! In His presence, I can do all things and be all that God has called me to be.

You protect them by your presence from what people plan against them. You shelter them from evil words.

—Psalm 31:20 NCV

Thou shall hide them in the secret of thy presence from the pride of man: thou shalt keep them secretly in a pavilion from the strife of tongues.

—Psalm 31:20 KJV

In a Gallup Poll as published in *Signs of the Times*, March 2013 issue, pollsters were asked the following question: Who's considered to be the most or least honest? The results are shown below:

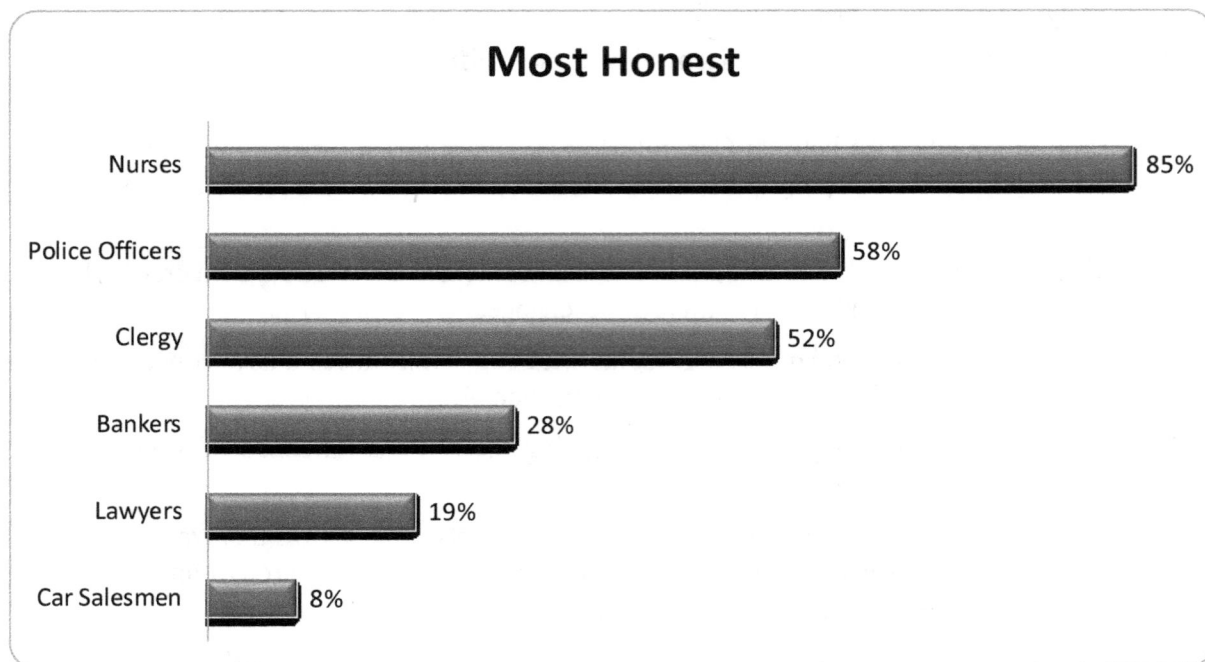

Most Honest

Nurses	85%
Police Officers	58%
Clergy	52%
Bankers	28%
Lawyers	19%
Car Salesmen	8%

In the shelter of His presence, He hides us:

There are six things that you will find in God's presence that you will not find anywhere else (KJV):

Hope—Psalm 118:13/21

Thou hast thrust sore at me that I might fall: but the LORD helped me. / I will praise thee: for thou hast heard me, and art become my salvation.

Love—Romans 5:5

And hope maketh not ashamed; because the love of God is shed abroad in our hearts by the Holy Ghost which is given unto us.

Protection—Psalm 31:20–21

> *Thou shalt hide them in the secret of thy presence from the pride of man: thou shalt keep them secretly in a pavilion from the strife of tongues. Blessed be the LORD for He hath shewed me his marvelous kindness in a strong city.*

Forgiveness—Isaiah 1:18

> *Come now, and let us reason together, saith the LORD: though your sins be as scarlet, they shall be as white as snow; though they be red like crimson, they shall be as wool.*

Direction—Isaiah 30:21

> *And thine ears shall hear a word behind thee, saying, This is the way, walk ye in it, when ye turn to the right hand, and when ye turn to the left.*

Joy—Psalm 16:11 and John 16:24

> *Thou wilt shew me the path of life: in thy presence is fulness of joy; at thy right hand there are pleasures for evermore.*

> *Hitherto have ye asked nothing in my name: ask, and ye shall receive, that your joy may be full.*

Your alternative is to trust in man, who changes frequently and ultimately abandons that plan and direction for the organization of company. It is abandoned because it did not work out as planned. Do not follow the scientific mind of man as he tries to figure out what God already knows. God commands us to love Him, hate sin, and give freely unto men. This includes giving of your resources, energy, knowledge, and time unto your fellow man and woman.

NOTES:

_____

_____

_____

_____

Traffic, Everyone Knows, is One of the Bigger Hassles of Modern Life

Walking by faith and not by sight can be a challenge during the typical commute to the office. Remember to focus on what God will have you to do rather than the circumstances surrounding that assignment. In an article entitled, "American Gridlock," by Phillip J. Longman, (*U.S. News and World*

Report, May 28, 2001), it was reported that *"traffic is making millions sick and tired. The bad news? It's going to get worse unless things change in a real big way."*

The advent of suburbia after the end of World War II led to a wave of commuters traveling into the big cities for office jobs. Since 1982, while the U.S. population has grown nearly twenty percent, the time Americans spend in traffic has jumped an amazing 236 percent. In major American cities, the length of the combined morning-evening rush hour has doubled, from under three hours in 1982 to almost six hours today. The result? The average driver now spends the equivalent of nearly a full workweek each year stuck in traffic.

That's not just lost time, but it's real money. Congestion costs Americans $78 billion per year in wasted fuel and lost time. That's an increase of thirty-nine percent since 1990. In New Jersey's Somerset County, where I once lived for six and one-half years, congestion costs the average licensed driver $2,100 a year. Further, I have personally experienced the dreadful two-hour door-to-door commute into midtown Manhattan. On occasion, the commute has been three hours—one way!

Congestion costs Americans nearly $80 billion
a year in wasted time and fuel.
Never mind the aggravation—UGH!

According to the most recent federal data, the amount of time that mothers spend behind the wheel increased by eleven percent just between 1990 and 1995, and there's every indication that the trend is continuing. Moms spend more time driving than they spend dressing, bathing, and feeding a child. Indicative of the growing concern about traffic among social conservatives, the Washington Family Council concludes in a report: "The long-term consequences of traffic reach far beyond simple economics; it seeps into the foundation of society—people and their families." It is reported that a clinical psychologist in Stockton, CA, just outside of San Francisco, counsels twelve to fifteen married couples each week, about half of which struggle with commuter-related stress. "They come in having only a dim awareness that commuting is the problem," says this psychologist. "Instead they are quarreling too much, and the affection's gone, and so is the sex."

Stressed-out commuters with little time for loved ones also don't have time for community involvement. Robert Putnam, a professor of public policy at Harvard University, has conducted extensive studies of the reasons behind Americans' decreasing involvement in social groups like the Parent-Teachers Association, church, recreational clubs, and political parties. Putnam's conclusion? Long commutes are a bigger reason than almost any demographic factor. This relationship can be plotted on a curve, Putnam says: For every ten minutes spent driving to work, involvement in community affairs drops by ten percent.

Annual delay per person, in hours

Hours	City
56	Los Angeles
53	Seattle
50	Houston
46	Washington, DC
45	Austin, Denver
44	St. Louis
42	San Francisco, Orlando, Miami, Boston, Nashville
41	Detroit
38	Minneapolis-St. Paul
34	Chicago, New York, Portland
33	Albuquerque
32	Charlotte
31	Phoenix

Source: Texas Transportation Institute—Texas A&M University.

NOTES:

_____

_____

_____

_____

What is Your Mountain Experience?

Mount Everest is the gold medal in the Olympic Games of mountaineering. At 29,028 feet, it is the tallest mountain in the world and represents the highest point of achievement for humans on the face of the earth. Sitting astride the border between Tibet to the north and Nepal to the south, Everest is a huge mass of black, forbidding rock and ice that dominates the landscape in every direction.

Meet Mr. John Amatt, a member of the first Canadian expedition to reach the summit of Mount Everest. In the introduction of his book entitled, *Straight to the Top and Beyond—Nine Keys for Meeting the Challenge of Changing Times* (1995), he encourages his readers with the following quote:

The challenge of change is forcing us to rethink our values and to rekindle the spirit of adventure. It will take courage, resourcefulness, and endurance to meet this challenge—the courage to try, to commit, and to take risks; the resourcefulness to be innovative and creative in finding new ways of doing old things; and the endurance to keep going when the going gets tough.

> *It is one of the great paradoxes of human existence that, by nature, we seek out comfort and predictability, using all of our financial resources and intellectual powers to devise technologies that will make our lives easier and less stressful. The paradox is that once*

we have created the comfort we desire, we must leave it all behind if we are to move forward toward future opportunity.

His parents, on their honeymoon in 1936, climbed in the Bernese Alps of Switzerland and, two years later, reached the summit of the 12,142-foot Wetterhorn, a mountain that his sister and he climbed when he was eighteen years old. Also in 1938, his parents were present in Grindlewald when the deadly north face of the Eiger was climbed for the first time, at that point—the most dramatic climb in history.

In chapter ten of his book, Mr. Amatt introduces a faith principle that he calls: *Adventure Attitude*. The nine keys of the *Adventure Attitude* are:

A — Adaptability

Change is not merely necessary to life. It is life! By the same token, life is adaptation.

—Alvin Toffler

D — Desire and Determination

You've got to hang on to your dreams. Great dreams don't happen overnight.

V — Vision and Values
Vision ... is the ability to:

- *Look to the past and learn from it;*
- *Look to the present and be attuned to it;*
- *Look to the future and be prepared for it.*

—Unknown

E — Experience

The only failure in life is when we fail to learn the lessons from our experience.

N — Natural Curiosity

If we're not pushing our limits, we're not discovering anything new.

T — Teamwork and Trust

Rarely do we achieve complete success in today's changing world without the help and support of others. The essence of teamwork is to identify and use the strengths of others to offset our own limitations, so that the strength of the team becomes greater than the sum of the individual parts.

U — Unlimited Optimism

Life is a leap of faith. There is no way that we can know what will happen tomorrow.

R — Risk-ability

The only limiting factor to our achievements in life is our fear of the unknown.

E — Exceptional Performance

Achievement is the constant process of going one step beyond your previous experience.

The thief cometh not, but for to steal, to kill, and to destroy: I am come that they might have life, and that they might have it more abundantly.

—John 10:10 KJV

The thief comes only in order to steal and kill and destroy. I came that they may have and enjoy life, and have it in abundance (to the full, till it [a]overflows).

—John 10:10 AMP

As the mountain climber gets an occasional exhilaration from climbing, we get the most out of life when we live for Christ. I see an application to the Christian's experience. Jesus did not call us to live the Christian life just to escape hell. It is not a life of minimum joy and fulfillment, but a life that is full and overflowing. Our purpose in following Christ should not be merely to avoid eternal punishment. If that is our primary motivation, we are missing the wonders and joys and victories of climbing higher and higher with Jesus.

Do not live minimally. Instead, live life to the maximum. Climb that mountain with confidence!

So we don't look at the troubles we can see now; rather, we fix our gaze on things that cannot be seen. For the things we see now will soon be gone, but the things we cannot see will last forever.

—2 Corinthians 4:18 NLT

While we look not at the things which are seen, but at the things which are not seen: for the things which are seen are temporal; but the things which are not seen are eternal.

—2 Corinthians 4:18 KJV

Bible Promises for Guidance (NIV)

Psalm 5:8—*Lead me, LORD, in your righteousness because of my enemies—make your way straight before me.*

Psalm 32:8—*I will instruct you and teach you in the way you should go; I will counsel you with my loving eye on you.*

2 Samuel 22:29—*You, LORD, are my lamp; the LORD turns my darkness into light.*

Psalm 73:24—*You guide me with your counsel, and afterward you will take me into glory.*

Romans 8:14—*For those who are led by the Spirit of God are the children of God.*

Proverbs 20:27—*The human spirit is[a] the lamp of the LORD that sheds light on one's inmost being.*

John 10:3–5—*The gatekeeper opens the gate for him, and the sheep* listen *to his voice. He calls his own sheep by name and leads them out.* [4] *When he has brought out all his own, he goes on ahead of them, and his sheep follow him because they know his voice.* [5] *But they will never follow a stranger; in fact, they will run away from him because they do not recognize a stranger's voice.*

Exodus 15:13—*In your unfailing love you will lead the people you have redeemed. In your strength you will guide them to your holy dwelling.*

Deuteronomy 32:10—*In a desert land he* found *him, in a barren and howling waste. He shielded him and cared for him; he guarded him as the apple of his eye.*

Nehemiah 9:19–20—*Because of your great compassion you did not abandon them in the wilderness. By day the pillar of cloud did not fail to guide them on their path, nor the pillar of fire by night to shine on the way they were to take.* [20] *You gave your good Spirit to instruct them. You did not withhold your manna from their mouths, and you gave them water for their thirst.*

Jeremiah 33:3—*Call to me and I will* answer *you and tell you great and unsearchable things you do not know.*

James 1:3—*Because you know that the testing of your faith produces perseverance.*

John 16:13—*But when he, the Spirit of truth, comes, he will guide you into all the truth. He will not speak on his own; he will speak only what he hears, and he will tell you what is yet to come.*

Luke 1:79—*To shine on those living in darkness and in the shadow of death, to guide our feet into* the path *of peace.*

Source: *Dare to Succeed: A Treasury of Inspiration and Wisdom for Life and Career* (Honor Books: 1994).

Questions for Personal Reflection or Group Discussion

1. Why does God require us to "Walk by Faith, Not by Sight?" Please support through discussion.

   _____

   _____

   _____

2. How do you handle traffic congestion? Describe some ways that you manage your time.

   _____

   _____

   _____

3. As a mentor, how do you select those mentees who request your time?

   _____

   _____

   _____

4. What is your most effective management style? Distinguish between "effective" and "preferred" styles.

   _____

   _____

   _____

5. What is/was your mountain experience?

   _____

   _____

   _____

food for thought

ON BELIEVING THE "UNSEEN"

As the clock ticked over to 08:01 PM on Wednesday, February 20, 2002, time read (only for sixty seconds) in perfect symmetry. To be more precise: 20:02, 2002. It was an event which has only ever happened once before. The last occasion that time read in such a symmetrical pattern was long before the days of the digital watch (or the 24-hour clock): 10:10 AM on January 10, 1001. And because the clock only goes up to 23:59, it is something that will never happen again.

Chapter Nine

Explain What You Mean (in Simple Terms)

"God loves you and He gave His only begotten Son for you. Come to Jesus ... "

—*Evangelist Billy Graham*, as he once concluded each of the thousands of local, regional, national, and international crusades with a call to Christ.

God did not give us a spirit that makes us afraid but a spirit of power and love and self-control.

—2 Timothy 1:7 NCV

For God hath not given us the spirit of fear, but of power, and of love, and of a sound mind.

—2 Timothy 1:7 KJV

Be a great communicator and eliminate all guesswork.

*T*he life of Evangelist Billy Graham is fascinating and phenomenal. I have listened to his sermons (*rhema*—the spoken word) and have read a number of his books including *Just As I Am—The Autobiography of Billy Graham* (1997), *Peace with God* (1953), *How to be Born Again* (1977), and *Billy Graham—God's Ambassador* (1999). His sermons were consistent and meaningful.

> *I have had the privilege of preaching the Gospel on every continent in most of the countries of the world. And I have found that when I present the simple message of the Gospel of Jesus Christ, with authority, quoting from the very Word of God—He takes that message and drives it supernaturally into the human heart.*

—Billy Graham

William Franklin Graham, Jr. was born in the downstairs bedroom in a frame farmhouse on November 7, 1918, three days before his father's thirtieth birthday. His parents called him Billy Frank. On Easter Sunday evening, 1937, he preached his first sermon at Bostwick Baptist Church, a country church near Palatka, Florida. His sermon lasted eight minutes. Today, he is one of the most recognizable figures in the world—a man who, for more than fifty years, has spoken in person to over 100 million people on six continents, in eighty-five countries, and in all of America's fifty states—more than any other man or woman in history. He has ministered to millions around the world, has counseled Presidents and Prime Ministers, and was the driving force behind the evangelical movement of the twentieth century. One of his most profound statements is: *"My one purpose in life is to help people find a personal relationship with God, which, I believe, comes through Jesus Christ."*

He is a man that consistently *means what he says.* God's Word says *"And I, if I be lifted up from the earth, will draw all men unto me"* (John 12:32). Evangelist Graham is forthright in his local, regional, national, and international crusades. He has spoken before millions of people, perhaps billions, in almost every country in the world. His sermons are:

- **Pure:** Clean hands and a pure heart Psalm 24:4

  "I am convinced that the greatest act of love we can ever perform for people is to tell them about God's love for them in Christ."

- **Genuine:** Not "puffed up," but humble 1 Peter 5:6

  "I would like to say that I am just one man among many that have come for this crusade. We have a whole team of people and most of us have been together for nearly fifty years. I'm introduced as though I'm doing it all. They have far greater skills than I have, they have far greater abilities and gifts than I have. But it's the Lord using this group of people along with the local churches to make Christ known to the community."

—The largest crowd at any event in the Los Angeles Memorial Coliseum was the 1963 Billy Graham crusade, with 134,254 inside and 20,000 more outside.

- **Focused:**   Knows his audience   Luke 19:10

"I had used from 25 to 100 passages of scripture with every sermon and learned that modern man will surrender to the impact of the Word of God."

- **Christ-centered:**   Always lifts up the name of Jesus   John 12:32

"I present a God who matters, and who makes claims on the human race. He is a God of love, grace, mercy, but also a God of judgment. When we break His moral laws we suffer; when we keep them we have inward peace and joy. I am calling for a revival that will cause men and women to return to their offices and shops to live out the teaching of Christ in their daily relationships. I preach a Gospel not of despair but of hope for the individual, hope for society, and hope for the world."

- **Simple:**   Everyone can understand   Proverbs 1:4

"God is a God of love, a God of mercy. He has the hairs of your head numbered ... He wants to come into your life and give you new hope."

—In October 1974, the largest crowd to attend an evangelistic service in the western hemisphere—225,000 people—filled Rio de Janeiro's Maracana Stadium.

- **Fearless and direct:**   An excellent communicator   Romans 12:13–18

"Nowhere in Mark 16:15—'Go ye into all the world, and preach the Gospel to every creature'—nor in any similar scripture did Christ command us to go only into the western or capitalist world. Nowhere did He say to exclude the Communist world."

—In July 1967, Billy Graham preached for the first time inside a Communist country— Yugoslavia. Technically it was not part of the Soviet bloc, yet these were Eastern Europe's first open-air evangelistic meetings since World War II.

- **Honest:**   Tells the truth   John 8:32

"I am convinced, through my travels and experiences, that people all over the world are hungry to hear the Word of God. As the people came to a desert place to hear John the Baptist proclaim, 'Thus saith the Lord,' so modern man in his confusions, frustrations, and bewilderment will come to hear the minister who preaches with authority."

—In March 1973, Johannesburg's Wanderers Stadium held 60,000 people, making it the largest multiracial gathering ever held in South Africa to that time.

- **Impactful:** Bold and uncompromising 1 John 4:17

"I had some hesitancy about taking this engagement because it was a variety show. However, I remembered that Jesus ate with publicans and sinners, even though He was denounced by the Pharisees. Here was an opportunity to give my testimony to 40 million Americans over NBC Television."

- **Moving:** Sincere and passionate in his delivery Matthew 5:16

"The real story of the crusades is not in the great choirs, the thousands in attendance, nor the hundreds of inquirers who are counseled. The real story is in the changes that have taken place in the hearts and lives of people."

—In June 1973, a record 1.1 million people made Yoido Plaza in Seoul, South Korea, Billy Graham's largest ever meeting held anywhere in the world.

- **Results-oriented:** Always concludes with a call to Christ Romans 10:9

"This is the spot that thousands of tourists think of as New York. Many foreign visitors judge America by Times Square. Some stare in wonderment at the blaze of lights; others hurry along streets to the theaters and places of amusement. Here in Times Square is the dope addict, the alcoholic, the harlot ... along with the finest citizens of the world. Let us tell the whole world tonight we Americans believe in God!"

—Closing Sermon of the New York Crusade, September 1, 1957

For He saith, I have heard thee in a time accepted, and in the day of salvation have I succoured thee: behold, now is the accepted time; behold, now is the day of salvation.

—2 Corinthians 6:2 KJV

He says, "When I showed you my favor, I heard you. On the day I saved you, I helped you." I tell you, now is the time God shows his favor. Now is the day he saves.

—2 Corinthians 6:2 NIRV

NOTES:

_____

_____

_____

_____

NOW *is the day of salvation!*

Dubbed the "world's most famous" preacher, Evangelist Billy Graham's four hundredth twelfth crusade took place in Dallas, Texas, before a record crowd at Texas Stadium that spilled out into an adjacent parking lot. Thousands of chairs were set up beneath a giant JumboTron screen. On this October evening, the frail, white-haired, eighty-four-year old evangelist slowly made his way to the pulpit to deliver the same simple message he has preached to more than 210 million people in over 180 countries over more than half a century: *"God loves you and He gave His begotten Son for you. Come to Jesus ... "*

Source: *U.S. News and World Report*, "A Christian Dynasty, How Billy Graham's Kids are Firing Up His Crusade," page 38.

Words to live by are just words,
unless we live by them.

Words are Powerful

Man's inability to communicate effectively is a result of his failure to listen skillfully and with understanding to another person.

—Carl Rogers, psychologist

Words, like eyeglasses, blur everything that they do not make clear.

—Joseph Joubert

Good communication is as stimulating as black coffee and just as hard to sleep after.

—Anne Morrow Lindbergh

Sticks & Stones ...

There is a popular saying that is mentioned regularly by children, men and women of all ages. It has to do with our futile attempts to demonstrate to others that their words do not affect us—especially the unkind ones. Although this saying is well known and often quoted, it is wrong. It goes like this: *"Sticks and stones may break my bones, but words will never hurt me."*

Unfortunately, this is not true. Words can either give life or cause death. They are so powerful, that *"word"* is used 679 times in *The Holy Bible*. *"Word's"* is used twice and *"words"* is used another 543 times! In the beginning, God, Himself, used words to create the earth (Genesis 1:3–31).

Creation of the World through the Spoken Word (KJV)

Day 1—God said, *"Let there be light and called the light Day and the darkness Night"* (verses 3–5).

Day 2—God said, *"Let there be a firmament in the midst of the waters and God called the firmament Heaven"* (verses 6–8).

Day 3—God said, *"Let the waters under the heaven be gathered together unto one place, and let the dry land appear..."* Thus, the earth and the seas were formed along with vegetation, herb yielding seed, and fruit (verses 9–13).

Day 4—God said, *"Let there be lights in the firmament of the heaven to divide the day from the night...and seasons and the sun, moon, and stars"* (verses 14–19).

Day 5—God said, *"Let the waters bring forth abundantly the moving creature that hath life, and fowl that may fly above the earth ... after their kind, and blessed them"* (verses 20–23).

Day 6—God said, *"Let the earth bring forth the living creature after his kind"* ... and God said, *"Let us make man in our image, after our likeness: and let them have dominion over the fish of the sea, and over the fowl of the air, and over the cattle, and over all the earth, and over every creeping thing that creepeth upon the earth"* ... And God blessed them, and God said unto them, *"Be fruitful, and multiply, and replenish the earth, and subdue it ..."* (verses 24–31).

Creation marks the absolute beginning of the temporal and material world. *"And God said,"* in verse 3, is the first of a highly structured series of succinct and formulaic sentences expressing the creative commands of God. Creation is accomplished by His word. Each command consists of the following:

An announcement	*"God Said"*
A creative command	*"Let there be"*
A summary word of accomplishment	*"And it was so"*
A descriptive word of accomplishment	*"The earth brought forth"*
A descriptive blessing	*"God blessed"*
An evaluative approval	*"It was good"*
A concluding temporal framework	**For example, numbering each day.**

In the book of John, we find scripture that further supports the supreme power of words. *"In the beginning was the Word, and the Word was with God, and the Word was God."* This signifies the perfect fellowship between God the Father and God the Son in eternity. "The Word was God" emphasizes distinction in the Godhead and this phrase stresses the essential unity. Jesus Christ was with God in the beginning and will continue to be throughout all eternity. "Word" means *logos*, which is one of the most important titles for Christ. The idea behind this title embodied God's revelation of Himself to humanity. Thus, God's plan to redeem mankind from the curse of the law was fulfilled by Jesus Christ. *"And the Word was made flesh, and dwelt among us, (and we beheld his glory, the glory as of the only begotten of the Father), full of grace and truth."*

Choose Your Words Carefully

God is continually reminding us, in His word, to be selective in how we speak to others on the job. Our choice of words can build up, but can also break down. Chapter three in the book of James offers Godly counsel on the dangers of the tongue. In this chapter of scripture, there are several lessons worth mentioning.

1. The tongue is the primary teaching tool and none of us can control it sufficiently (verses 1–2).

2. The tongue represents a system (the world) of iniquity that sets on fire the whole course of life, and is even set on fire by Satan (verse 6).

3. We are made in the image of God. To curse people and yet bless God is inconsistent. Though the fall of mankind has marred that image or likeness, it still exists (verse 9).

4. Godly wisdom is necessary in a teacher for effective communication. The teacher must exhibit a meek and practical application of the truth. You cannot teach what you do not live (verse 13)!

5. Two wisdoms are expounded by teachers. The one from God is pure and promotes peace, ending in righteousness. However, the other is demonic and natural, visible in the teacher as jealousy and ambition. The result of such teaching is evil living and confusion (verses 14 to 18).

That ye may be blameless and harmless, the sons of God, without rebuke, in the midst of a crooked and perverse nation, among whom ye shine as lights in the world.

—Philippians 2:15 KJV

That you may show yourselves to be blameless and guileless, innocent and uncontaminated, children of God without blemish (faultless, unrebukable) in the midst of a crooked and wicked generation [spiritually perverted and perverse], among whom you are seen as bright lights (stars or beacons shining out clearly) in the [dark] world.

—Philippians 2:15 AMP

To shine as lights in this world, we (Christians) must be blameless—no finger of accusation can justly be pointed at us—and harmless—morally pure. If we are participating in partying and bickering, as the Philippians were, this cannot be held true. As the sons of God, who live in the midst of a crooked and perverse nation (generation), the Apostle Paul teaches us to be without rebuke. That is, without incurring spiritual damage.

Our proper place as Christians is amongst the lost. For only in such a position can true witness be borne and influence for the gospel to be effectively exerted. We shine as lights in the world if we remain *without rebuke* in that we suffer no moral damage by contact with the unsaved. Just as a star is readily noticeable in the dark sky, so healthy Christian lives stand out in testimony among the lost and give credence to one's witness.

> *His lord said unto him, Well done, thou good and faithful servant: thou hast been faithful over a few things, I will make thee ruler over many things: enter thou into the joy of thy lord.*

—Matthew 25:21 KJV

> *His lord said to him, 'Well done, good and faithful servant; you were faithful over a few things, I will make you ruler over many things. Enter into the joy of your lord.'*

—Matthew 25:21 NKJV

This scripture confirms continued service because of good stewardship over a few things. Be a great communicator along the way!

NOTES:

_____

_____

_____

_____

What Type Are You?

"There are two types of people in the world," someone once said, "those who come into a room and say, 'Here I am!' and those who come in say, 'Ah, there *you* are!'" How different are these two approaches!

Wouldn't it be great to be known as the second type of person? Someone others love to have around? Someone who displays the love of Christ openly, honestly, and unashamedly?

The New Testament of *The Holy Bible* gives us some practical suggestions about becoming the kind of person who demonstrates Christ's love. We are told to give preference to one another (Romans 12:10), edify one another (Romans 14:19), care for one another (1 Corinthians 12:25), serve one another (Galatians 5:13), bear one another's burdens (Galatians 6:2), forgive one another (Colossians 3:13), comfort one another (1 Thessalonians 5:11), and pray for one another (James 5:16).

There should only be one kind of Christian: the "love one another" kind. What type are you?[12]

Final messages of hope and advice on being a better communicator from one of the world's greatest communicators:

> As Christians we have a responsibility toward the poor, the oppressed, the downtrodden, and the many innocent people around the world who are caught in wars, natural disasters, and situations beyond their control. The Bible has more than a thousand verses related to helping our neighbor in their time of need. Jesus said in Matthew 25:40, "When you helped these my brothers, you were helping me."

> Courage is contagious. When a brave person takes a stand, the spines of others are stiffened."

> Someday you will read or hear that Billy Graham is dead. Don't you believe a word of it! I shall be more alive then than I am now. I will just have changed my address. I will have gone into the presence of God.

—Evangelist Billy Graham

---

[12] RBC Ministries, *Our Daily Bread*, December 4, 2002.

Questions for Personal Reflection or Group Discussion

1. Effective communication requires that the person on the other end of the conversation receive your message. Are you an effective communicator? Explain.

_____

_____

_____

2. View a film clip of a Billy Graham's crusade of your choice. How does he deliver the Word of God that encourages his listeners to respond?

_____

_____

_____

3. How do you set the atmosphere through the words that you use?

_____

_____

_____

4. Read Philippians 2:15. Discuss its meaning and implications.

_____

_____

_____

5. Do you encourage (build up) or discourage (tear down) with your communication style?

_____

_____

_____

food for thought

FOR EXPRESSION

Bill Gates gave advice to a high school graduating class at Mount Whitney High School in Visalia, California entitled, "Rules for Life." They are his eleven rules of living—life principles that young people <u>will not</u> learn in school:

1. Life is not fair—get used to it.
2. The world won't care about your self-esteem. The world will expect you to accomplish something BEFORE you feel good about yourself.
3. You will NOT make $40,000 a year right out of high school. You won't be a vice-president with a car phone until you earn both.
4. If you think your teacher is tough, wait until you get a boss.
5. Flipping hamburgers is not beneath your dignity. Your grandparents had a different word for burger flipping—they called it opportunity.
6. If you mess up, it's not your parents' fault, so don't whine about your mistakes, learn from them.
7. Before you were born, your parents weren't as boring as they are now. They got that way from paying your bills, cleaning your clothes and listening to you talk about how cool you are. So before you save the rain forest from the parasites of your parents' generation, try de-lousing the closet in your own room.
8. Your school may have done away with winners and losers, but life has not. In some schools, they have abolished failing grades and they'll give you as many times as you want to get the right answer. This doesn't bear the slightest resemblance to ANYTHING in real life.
9. Life is not divided into semesters. You don't get summers off and very few employees are interested in helping you find yourself. Do that on your own time.
10. Television is NOT real life. In real life people actually have to leave the coffee shop and go to jobs.
11. Be nice to nerds. Chances are you'll end up working for one!

Conclusion

*T*hrough its subtitle, *Called to be **Light** in the Workplace*, this book challenges its readers to be *light* on their respective job(s) in each of the three phases of career progression: Entry-level (trainee or intern), journey-man level (middle manager), and senior level (executive or mentor). God's Word ministers how to encourage others at work and influence positive change in the midst of frequently dysfunctional places of employment. Through the lives of Jesus, Dr. Martin Luther King, Jr., Evangelist Billy Graham, and many other recognizable and unrecognizable names, excellence in their jobs raised the level of productivity of others. Thus, this book impacts the lives of blue- and white-collar workers. It is systematically divided into three parts, with three chapters each. Supported by the scriptures throughout, the central theme of each chapter focuses on specific ways to let our *light* shine and to *Give God the Glory!* while at work every day.

Focus your efforts, at each phase during your career, on the central theme of each chapter. Each of us has an important role to play to ensure that our colleagues, peers, associates, bosses, subordinates, and strangers know that God is a real God! He resides *in* us, therefore, He resides at our places of employment. He resides everywhere that we go—Represent Him well!

PART ONE—The Formative Years ... *in the beginning*

1.   Chapter One—Growth
        Central theme: Be open to *learn* and *grow*.

2.   Chapter Two—Development
        Central theme: Develop skills along the way. *Never stop learning.*

3.   Chapter Three—Maturity
        Central theme: *Responsibility and accountability* are measures of maturity.

PART TWO—The Journeyman Years ... *from learning to leading*

4.   Chapter Four—Applying What You Now Know
        Central theme: *Put to practice* what you have learned.

5.   Chapter Five—Become What You Have Learned
        Central theme: *Cultivate your skills* with patience. Be fair and cordial as you progress.

6.   Chapter Six—What Makes a Leader?
        Central theme: *Service* to others makes you a great leader.

Glory is mentioned 395 times throughout *The Holy Bible*. It must be quite important to God that we understand how to **Give God the Glory!** that He desires and deserves. As God's chosen children—ambassadors for Christ—we are the visible manifestation of an invisible God. It is therefore crucial that Christians (Christ-like ones) represent God in a manner that is holy, righteous, and distinctively different from what the world wants to teach us. Think about how you will let your *light* shine on your job and how you will make a positive impact. No matter where you work or what type of work that you do, always **Give God the Glory!**

Concluding Prayer

Dear Heavenly Father,

I come to you in the precious and matchless name of Jesus, even the Christ, whose I am and whom I serve. Thank you Father for the wonderful opportunity and privilege to write about Your glory in my life. You are a sovereign God who is in all places, knows all things, and is infinite in power. You are the source of my life.

Father, I pray that through the words of this book, and its message, that you touch each reader and speak to them specifically concerning their issues at work. Teach them how to carefully handle each situation through Your word. Bless them indeed and give them insight into Godly principles as it relates to their livelihood. Teach them more than just how to earn a living through their respective jobs, but teach them how to live. Your word says that *"And I, if I be lifted up from the earth, I will draw all men unto me."* Prick their hearts to have a desire to know You and to develop a closer walk with You.

Demonstrate to us Father, through Your Spirit, how to be *light* on our jobs. Your word says, *"But seek ye first the Kingdom of God, and His righteousness, and all these things shall be added unto you."* Please continue to nurture and provide for us by continually reminding us that You will take care us of in all situations. Our provisions are cared for even before we know what to ask for. For that, I thank You.

I ask that You continue to empower and strengthen me to continue to fulfill the vision for *Writing for the Lord* Ministries and to always use me as your willing earthen vessel. I lift this prayer up to You Father, in the name of Jesus, whose I am and whom I serve.

Amen.

Morning Prayer

My Heavenly Father, as I enter this work place, I bring your presence with me.
I speak Your peace, Your grace, Your mercy, and Your perfect order into this office.
I acknowledge Your power over all that will be spoken, thought, decided, and done within these walls
Lord.

I thank You for the gifts You have blessed me with.
I commit to using them responsibly in Your honor.
Give me a fresh supply of strength to do my job.
Anoint my projects, ideas, and energy so that even my smallest accomplishment may bring You glory.

Lord, when I am confused, guide me.
When I am weary, energize me.
When I am burned out, infuse me with the *light* of the Holy Spirit.
May the work that I do and the way I do it bring faith, joy, and smiles to all that I come in contact with
today.

And oh Lord, when I leave this place, give me traveling mercy.
Bless my family and home to be in order as I left it.
Lord, I thank you for everything You've done, everything You're doing, and everything You're going to
do.

In the Name of Jesus I pray, with much love and thanksgiving …
Amen.

—Author Unknown

Test Your Common Sense

Answers

1. (a) Cross with caution. This is what you do routinely at intersections that don't have walk lights (and never had walk lights). The present intersection is now one of them.

2. (b) Buy the unfancy kind. You're short of cash and you love all varieties of tuna equally, so you shouldn't spend more for any one of them.

3. (a) The warmer one. If you buy the one that looks much better, you will still need a warm winter coat.

4. (a) Go to the interview. You need a job, and canceling won't help you get one. Your hair will only grow longer.

5. (a) Repair the shoes. They'll be just as good as new shoes for only half of what it would cost to buy another pair. Your financial circumstances are not significant.

6. (b) Don't guess. You have two choices for action. One carries a penalty, and one does not. If you choose the action with a penalty, your score will likely suffer: That's why you were warned.

7. (b) The one with the view of the flashing neon sign. If the question had noted that you love parks, you would have chosen the apartment with the park view.

Did you know that Marilyn vos Savant is listed in the Guinness Book of World Records Hall of Fame *for "Highest IQ?"*

How to Be a Godly Employee

Based upon the Ten Commandments

by: Drew M. Crandall, President, Northeast Christians at Work ©1998

1. **Trust in God only**. Trust in no one but God. People will disappoint you. God created you, He loves you, and has a wonderful plan for your life. He is too good to do wrong, and too wise to make a mistake, even when the "fur is flying." Let His peace abide in you. *(Proverbs 3:5–6)*

2. **Worship God only**. Don't make your career, your company, or your boss a god. If you do, you will provoke Him to jealousy and will end up fighting Him. In fact, He may hinder you from achieving what you want until you are broken of the idolatry. *(Exodus 20:5)*

3. **Use God's name reverently**. Don't swear! Clean words come out of a clean heart. If your co-workers know you're religious, but they hear the Lord's name used in vain, cursing and swearing coming out of your mouth, you will give the appearance of being a hypocrite. *(Matthew 15:17–19)*

4. **Work six days and rest on the seventh**. Before you beg for more vacation time, ask yourself a couple of questions: do you honor the Sabbath? God has already given you 52 days (over seven weeks) of time off. Are your expectations at work, vacation, and retirement realistic, or are you living in fantasyland? By resting one day per week, you can avoid burnout. *(Genesis 3:17–19)*

5. **Respect and obey your boss**. You should respect and obey your boss, because you don't know what it's like to be in his/her shoes. Plus, your ultimate boss is the Lord. Serve Him faithfully on the job, and He will bless you! However, if your boss commands you to do something illegal or immoral, you must make a stand and obey God rather than man. *(Ephesians 6:5–8)*

6. **Protect and respect human life**. Emotional, mental, spiritual, and physical manipulation, abuse, and violence have no place in the workplace … or any place. You do not have the right to use and abuse your boss, your co-workers, your employees, your customers, or your suppliers. *(2 Thessalonians 3:1–2)*

7. **Be true to your spouse**. If you're not getting the kind of attention and affection that you feel you deserve at home, it's common to seek it with someone at work. Honor your wedding vows by avoiding company romances! They are very real, very tempting, and very common. They're also very wrong and very destructive. *(Matthew 19:8–9)*

8. **Don't take what belongs to others**. Stealing at work can take many forms. You can choose to steal materials, money, time, productivity, and joy from your employer, co-workers, customers, and suppliers. Don't remove your integrity by stealing. *(2 Corinthians 7:1–2)*

9. **Do not lie about others**. Do not fabricate stories about your boss or co-workers, and spread gossip for the sake of company politics. You're here to be salt and light, not pepper and darkness! Truth always rises to the surface, and eventually you will be ashamed and rebuked if you lie. *(2 Peter 2:10–13)*

10. **Be satisfied with what you have**. Contentment doesn't mean that you can't pursue God-given goals … but it does mean that you're content with what He has provided you with day by day. Contentment is a rare quality in today's culture … but it is extremely liberating! Materialism, striving for rank, and discontent leads to emotional, mental, financial, and spiritual bondage. *(1 Timothy 6:6–11)*

Psalm 23 (For the Work Place)

The Lord is my real boss, and I shall not want.

He gives me peace, when chaos is all around me.

He gently reminds me to pray and do all things without murmuring and complaining.

He reminds me that HE is my source (and not my job).

He restores my sanity every day and guides my decisions that I might honor Him in all that I do.

Even though I face an absurd amount of e-mails, system crashes, unrealistic deadlines, budget cutbacks, gossiping co-workers, discriminating supervisors, and an aging body that doesn't cooperate every morning, I still will not stop—for He is with me!

His presence, His peace, and His power will see me through.

He raises me up, even when they fail to promote me.

He claims me as His own, even when the company threatens to let me go.

His faithfulness and love are better than any bonus check.

His retirement plan beats every 401k there is!

When it's all said and done, I'll be working for Him a whole lot longer and for that,

I BLESS HIS NAME!

—Author Unknown

A Reader's Guide: A Conversation with Kevin Wayne Johnson

Facilitated by Lynn Pinder, Founder/Director, Christian Authors on Tour

Interview of Pastor Kevin W. Johnson

(Introduction)

FEMALE VOICE: Thank you for tuning into the Christian Authors on Tour Blog Talk Radio Show. Sit back and enjoy inspirational interviews with Christian fiction and non-fiction authors from around the world who are on fire for God, and committed to using writing as a ministry tool. Feel free to follow our show at: www.blogtalkradio.com/ christianauthorsontour or like our Facebook page: thechristianauthorsontour blogtalkradioshow.

(Blog Talk Radio Show begins)

MS. PINDER: Good evening, good evening, good evening. You are listening to the Christian Authors on Tour Blog Talk Radio Show. This is one of your co-hosts, Lynn Pinder, and I am so excited. I know if you're listening live, you're wondering, why are they on the air on a Sunday. Well, this is a special broadcast; we're only going to be on the air for 15 minutes.

And we have a powerful man of God who is no stranger to Christian Authors on Tour; he's actually one of the co-host of the Christian Authors on Tour Blog Talk Radio Show. But he has something awesome happening, and we want to just give him an opportunity to share that with the listening audience.

But let me just give you a little bit of background. Christian Authors on Tour is a group of Christian authors from all around the country who use writing as a tool for Christian ministry. And this Blog Talk Radio Show is a venue for Christian authors from all over the world to share how God is using them in their call to use writing as a tool for Christian ministry.

Our guest author tonight is none other than Pastor Kevin Wayne Johnson. He is the founder of *Writing for the Lord* Ministries, and the author of the **Give God the Glory!** book series. Pastor Johnson, he is the winner of seventeen literary and media awards, and he's also a returning faculty member of the 2013 Greater Philly Christian Writer's Conference. On September first, Pastor Johnson will release a new book titled, "Called to be Light in the Workplace: A Workbook."

And I'm so excited tonight for this special broadcast to introduce the psalm and to just bring back for others, Pastor Kevin Wayne Johnson.

Hey, Pastor Johnson, how are you?

PASTOR JOHNSON: I'm doing well, Lynn. Thank you so much for this awesome opportunity. It's always a pleasure to be with you again.

MS. PINDER: Well, you know, I'm excited to be able to share with our listening audience, you know, this new writing project that you're working on. And I want you to go ahead and just tell the listening audience about the Give God the Glory! series and what it's all about, and this new book that you have coming out on September first.

PASTOR JOHNSON: Absolutely, absolutely. Well, this is going to be book number eight in the Give God the Glory! series that was birthed twelve years ago. We began with one title, subtitled, "Know God and Do the Will of God Concerning Your Life," self-published, as with most first-time authors. And the book was picked up for national distribution within about two-and-a-half to three months, which was really, really an awesome thing.

Once that assignment was completed, God gave me more information about the series of books that should follow and spoke very clearly to me about writing that core message; give God the glory, which means put God first and foremost in everything that we do because He is our source.

Focusing on five key areas would really be the nucleus, and the genesis, and the heart and soul of this series of non-fiction books. So we started out with relationships; relationships one to another and with our heavenly Father.

And then the very next book in the series was subtitled, "Called to be *Light* in the Workplace." And what we do in this book is we really capture the essence of what it means to give God the glory while we're at work. And it doesn't really matter what the vocation is, it doesn't matter what the job is, it doesn't really matter what we do for a living. You can be a nurse, you can be a VP of finance, you can be a fire chief, you could be a chef—it really doesn't matter. But the bottom line is to usher in the love of God in the workplace to make it a much better place.

And so we specifically address three key areas. Entry level; when we're coming into the workplace as young individuals just coming out of college or maybe even just coming out of high school. There are things that we can do to glean wisdom from those who are older than us chronologically in age.

Once we get to that middle level in our career, approximately ten to fifteen years, God is looking to place us strategically in the workplace to, not only help those who are coming up behind us, but glean wisdom from those that are ahead of us.

And then in the third area, it happens to be once we reach that supervisor, managerial, senior executive level. How does God use us in the workplace to make it a much better place based upon the wisdom that we have gained, the experience that we now have captured? And how can we nurture those that are coming up behind us at that senior level as we look forward to retirement and moving onto our next season in life.

And so that was the impetus of the second book in the series which was released worldwide ten years ago in 2003. Hence, fast forward ten years to today, 2013; that same book has now been expanded and revised.

We've incorporated additional versions of the Bible to add clarity because we're reaching an even wider audience now. And we've transitioned the book from six by nine to now, eight-and-a-half by eleven. So, it's an actually a larger book, and it's a workbook. So it's intended to really help all of us to really understand through study, through prayer, through meditation what it really means, in a workbook format, to give God the glory in those key areas; entry level, journeymen level or mid-year level, and then also at the senior levels when we transition into supervisors, and managers, and senior executives. Because God uses us strategically, and in certain ways based upon our gifts, in different ways in each of those three phases.

And so I'm very, very happy to let all of our listening audience know that on the first of July of this year, we will be launching our ninety-day pre-publication campaign worldwide. For ninety days the book will be available for half-price, $7.50, prior to the worldwide release at the regular retail price of $15.00 on Labor Day weekend.

And the reason we're doing that is we really want people to have an opportunity to get the book in their hands to share it, not only with their church groups, but within their community, within their home, within the workplace in particular, to really spread this message; giving God the glory, because all of us are called to be light in the workplace.

And the core message that people are going to find from page one to page two hundred, the core message is, is that our *light* helps to illuminate and dispel and cause to go away any darkness that's happening into the workplace. And the darkness creeps into the workplace is because folks that are in leadership positions are out of place. And so, if we're not exhibiting servant leadership, as Jesus taught us in His Word, then everything else in the workplace is out of whack.

So that's what this is all about. It's going to be a ninety-day campaign kicking off on the first of July. Our goal is to sell a certain number of copies at half-price. And then on Labor Day weekend—actually, September the second, the book will be released worldwide at the regular price of $15.00.

And we're doing this, number one; we want it to be affordable to everyone, and we want to reach as many people as we can. It's going to be an awesome campaign. We're going to be doing a lot of social media, I'm going to be present at a number of different venues across the country for that ninety-day period doing a lot of travel, a lot of book signings, a lot of discussions, etcetera.

And we're going to make it widely available to as many people as we can reach. Because when it's all said and done, nobody wants to go to their job every day to be miserable. We want to go to our jobs every day and enjoy the process, and learn, and grow, and develop, and then become that senior leader that God has intended us to be, using the golden rule in the workplace;

do unto others as you would have them to do unto you. There's not enough of that going on. So God and I had a conversation about that. And I told God, I said, "I am willing to be an earthen vessel to help make change in that area." And so we're very, very excited about it.

MS. PINDER: All right, all right. So Pastor Johnson, if people want to purchase the pre-released copy, how can they do that? Can you give your website information, your contact information?

PASTOR JOHNSON: Absolutely. The primary way, and what we're really encouraging everyone to do, is to go directly to the website. So the Christian-based publishing company that we established twelve years ago is *Writing for the Lord* Ministries. And that's where you find all of the Give God the Glory! book series, plus the other books we author as well and publish under that logo.

And so, the website is: www.writingforthelord.com, and writingforthelord.org. We have two domains; both domains will get you to the same website. And if you just go on site and go online to the bookstore that's online, you'll be able to get copies there. Of course the books will be available through Amazon.com as well. And it will also be available as an e-book; we're going to give people an opportunity to download it as an e-book as well. And they can go to smashwords.com to see the plethora of the **Give God the Glory!** books there as well.

So we're going to—we have a number of different ways that people can get access. But primarily through the website and through Amazon.com, and through our distributor. Our distributor is based out of Elizabeth Town, Tennessee. Send the Light Distributors; we'll be working in collaboration with them as well. That's the primary venue for the bookstores to get access to the book. But the readers who don't really need to go the bookstore, they can order it directly; can just go directly to the website: writingforthelord.com.

MS. PINDER: Awesome, awesome. And we only have a few minutes left, and so I want you to share with our listening audience, you already talked about how God basically gave you the mandate and the direction to write the book. Can you talk a little bit about, you know, what you hope readers will get, that one takeaway that they'll get from actually reading this new book series.

PASTOR JOHNSON: Yeah. I want people in the workplace, especially those individuals who are trusted with the awesome responsibility of managing and supervising others, I would like to see us transcend from mandating, dictating, and threatening, and start to transition towards servant leadership.

When you develop relationships with people, they're more likely to get the task done without you having to beg and pull and threaten. And so, having had experienced both ends, I know what works and what doesn't work. Having been a manager and supervisor and executive in the workplace for the past fifteen–sixteen years, I know what I've applied with my staff and what really, really works.

People appreciate being treated right, fairly, and equitably when they come to their job every day because they're there for such a long period of time; forty plus hours a week is a long time.

And so that's the core message that I would like people to take away. And when you do that, it's from our good works that we find in the book of Matthew that glorifies our Father in heaven. And so, that's really what it's all about. Again, I said it earlier, the golden rule; just do unto others as you would have them to do unto you. And then together we can make this world a much, much better place.

MS. PINDER: All right, all right. Well, thank you so much, Pastor Johnson for being on the broadcast tonight, not as a co-host but as our special guest. And I want you to give your website information one more time.

PASTOR JOHNSON: Okay. Well, the e-mail is Kevin@writingforthelord.com. And then the web address is www.writingforthelord.com, or writingforthelord.org; they'll get you to the same place. And you'll see all the information about the ministry, all the different speaking events that are going on, and all of the information about the books. And they're easy to purchase and each of the books in the series has a slightly different subtitle, so depending on what the readers are looking for in particular, there's a book in there for you.

So I look forward to an opportunity to connect with a lot of great people for the remainder of this year and beyond. And like we've been writing for the last twelve years, together let's *Give God the Glory!*

MS. PINDER: Amen, amen. Well, listening audience, you have been listening to the Christian Authors on Tour Blog Talk Radio Show. That was Pastor Kevin Wayne Johnson. This was a special fifteen-minute special broadcast, and we want you to definitely support Pastor Johnson. Go out; make sure you purchase copies of his book. But most importantly, we want you to read the most important book in the world, and that's the Holy Bible. You find a scripture and you hide it in your heart, and you live it.

Good night, everybody. Goodnight, Pastor Johnson.

PASTOR JOHNSON: All right, good night. Thank you so much. God bless you.

Selected Bibliography and Recommended Reading

Miner, Margaret and Hugh Rawson. *A Dictionary of Quotations from The Bible*. New York: Penguin Group [A Signet Book], 1990.

Abrahamson, Vickie, Mary Meehan, and Larry Samuel. *The Future Ain't What it Used to Be, The 40 Cultural Trends Transforming Your Job, Your Life, Your World*. New York: Riverhead Books, 1997.

Adams, Scott. *The DILBERT Future—Thriving on Stupidity in the 21st Century*. New York: HarperBusiness, 1997.

Amatt, John. *Straight to the Top and Beyond—Nine Keys for Meeting the Challenge of Changing Times*. Alberta, Canada: Kan-Sport Publishing, 1995.

Begley, Sharon. "God & the Brain, How We're Wired for Spirituality." *Newsweek*, May 7, 2001.

Bell, Michel A. *Managing God's Time: Personal Effectiveness Improvement*. Winepress Publishing, 2004.

Bernstein, Albert J. Ph.D. and Sydney Craft Rozen. *Sacred Bull—The Inner Obstacles that Hold You Back at Work and How to Overcome Them*. New York: John Wiley & Sons, Inc., 1994.

Blank, Warren. *THE 108 Skills of Natural Born Leaders*. New York: AMACOM, 2001.

Bottke, Alison with Cheryl Hutchings and Jennifer Devlin. *God Answers Prays—Military Edition*. Eugene, OR: Harvest House, 2005.

Bugbee, Bruce and Don Cousins with Wendy Seidman. *Network Participants Guide—Revised*. Grand Rapids, MI: Zondervan, 2005.

Crouch, Van. *Dare to Succeed: A Treasury of Inspiration and Wisdom for Life and Career*. Tulsa, OK: Honor Books, 1994.

Dobson, James Dr. *Focus on the Family* Newsletter.

Dockery, Karen, Johnnie Godwin, and Phyllis Godwin. *The Student Bible Dictionary*. Uhrichsville, OH: Barbour Publishing, Inc., 2000.

"Women Who Choose not to Smash the Glass Ceiling." *Financial Times,* April 6–7, 2002.

"Indonesia Thrives on Peace and Quiet." *Financial Times,* July 8, 2002.

FRONTLINES—Snapshot of History, written by award-winning Reuters journalists. London: Pearson Education Limited, 2001.

God's Little Instruction Book for the Class of 2002. Tulsa, OK: Honor Books, 2002.

Good Stuff, A Monthly Collection of Insights & Inspiration. Malvern, PA: Progressive Business Publications.

Gore, Al. *From Red Tape to Results, Creating A Government That Works Better and Costs Less—The Report of the National Performance Review*. New York, NY: Plume, 1993.

Newell Jochum, Elizabeth. "The Power of Frequent Career-Building Chats." *Government Executive—* Management Matters, November 14, 2012.

Newell Jochum, Elizabeth. "Rethinking To-Do Lists." *Government Executive*—Management Matters, December 5, 2012.

Graham, Billy. *God's Ambassador, A Lifelong Mission of Giving Hope to the World*. San Diego: Tehabi Books, 1999.

Gunther, Marc. "God and Business, the Surprising Quest for Spiritual Renewal in the American Workplace." *Fortune Magazine*, July 16, 2001.

Harvey, Eric and Alexander Lucia. *Walking the Talk Together—Sharing the Responsibility for Bringing Values to Life*. Dallas: Performance Publishing, 1998.

Johnson, Charles and Bob Adelman. *KING, The Photobiography of Martin Luther King, Jr.* New York: Penguin Putnam, Inc., 2000.

Johnston, William B. and Arnold E. Packer. *Workforce 2000, Work and Workers for the Twenty-First Century*. Indianapolis, IN: Hudson Institute, 1987.

King, Martin Luther, Jr., *I Have A Dream—Anniversary Edition*. San Francisco: HarperCollins Publishers, 1963, 1993.

Laurie, Greg. *The Great Compromise*. Minneapolis: World Wide Publications, 1994.

Leeds, Dorothy. *The 7 Powers of Questions, Secrets to Successful Communication in Life and at Work*. New York: Perigee Books, 2000.

Loden, Marilyn and Judy B. Rosener. *Workforce America! Managing Employee Diversity as a Vital Resource*. Homewood, IL: Business One Irwin, 1991.

Maxwell, John C. *Developing the Leaders Around You—How to Help Others Reach their Full Potential*. Nashville: Thomas Nelson Publishers, 1995.

Malone, Carlos L., Sr. *The Road to Purpose: The Journey Beyond Potential*. Newberg, PA: Milestones International Publishers, 2011.

Mecum, Shelly. *God's Photo Album, How We Looked for God and Saved Our School*. New York: HarperCollins Publishers, Inc., 2001.

Nance, Terry. *God's Armor Bearer: How to Serve God's Leaders*. Tulsa, OK: Harrison House, 1990.

Positive Community, The Magazine. Irvington, NJ.

Pound, Ron, and Price Pritchett. *A Survival Guide to the Stress of Organizational Change*. Dallas: Pritchett & Associates, Inc.

Pound, Ron, and Price Pritchett. *Business as Unusual—The Handbook for Managing and Supervising Organizational Change*. Dallas: Pritchett & Associates, Inc., 1995.

PriceWaterHouseCoopers *Telecom Direct* Newsletter.

Pritchett, Price Ph.D. *Culture Shift—The Employee Handbook for Changing Corporate Culture*. Dallas: Pritchett & Associates, Inc.

Pritchett, Price Ph.D. *Resistance—Moving Beyond the Barriers to Change*. Dallas: Pritchett & Associates, Inc.

Pritchett, Price. *The Employee Handbook of New Work Habits for a Radically Changing World—13 Ground Rules for Job Success in the Information Age*. Pritchett Rummler-Brache.

Pritchett, Price Ph.D. *The Ethics of Excellence*. Dallas: Pritchett & Associates, Inc.

Rath, Tom. *Strengths Finder 2.0*. New York: Gallup Press, 2007.

RBC Ministries, *Our Daily Bread—For Personal and Family Devotions*.

Schmidt, Michael A. *Tired of Being Tired, Overcoming Chronic Fatigue & Low Energy*. Berkeley, CA: Frog, Ltd., 1995.

September 11—A Testimony. London: Pearson Education Limited, 2002.

Strong, James. *Strong's Exhaustive Concordance of the Bible*. Peabody, MA: Hendrickson Publishers.

Taulbert, Clifton. *Eight Habits of the Heart: Embracing the Values that Build Strong Families and Communities*. New York: Penguin Books, 1997.

The Holy Bible, The New Open Bible Study Edition, King James Version Study Bible. Nashville, TN: Thomas Nelson Publishers, 1990.

The King James Study Bible, King James Version. Nashville, TN: Thomas Nelson Publishers, 1999.

"Great Discoveries, An Amazing Journey Through Space and Time." *Time Magazine*—Special Collector's Edition. New York: Time Books, 2001.

The Sunday Star-Ledger Newspaper.

The Wall Street Journal Newspaper.

USA Today Newspaper.

"Traffic, How it's Changing Life in America." *U.S. News & World Report*, May 28, 2001.

"A Christian Dynasty—How Billy Graham's Kids are Firing up His Crusade." *U.S. News & World Report*, December 23, 2002.

"Who We Were, Who We Are, How an Epic Century Changed a Nation." *U.S. News & World Report*, August 6, 2001.

Vines, W.E., Merrill F. Unger, and William White, Jr. *Complete Expository Dictionary of Old and New Testament Words*. Nashville, TN: Thomas Nelson Publishers, 1984, 1996.

Welch, Jack with Robert Slater. *Get Better or Get Beaten, 29 Leadership Secrets from GE's Jack Welch*. New York: McGraw- Hill Companies, 2001.

What Would Jesus Do? Uhrichsville, OH: Barbour Publishing, Inc., 1920.

Williams, Pat, with Jim Denney. *The Leadership Wisdom of Solomon: 28 Essential Strategies for Leading with Integrity*. Cincinnati, OH: Standard Publishing, 2010.

Zander, Rosamund Stone and Benjamin Zander. *The Art of Possibility, Transforming Professional and Personal Life*. Boston: Harvard Business School Press, 2000.

About the Author

With the fundamental belief that *God uses ordinary people to accomplish extraordinary things*, Pastor Kevin Wayne Johnson lives to spread the gospel of Jesus Christ. His passion is reflected through his national best-selling book series *Give God the Glory!* (that earned eighteen literary awards from 2001 to 2013, and are all published through his Christian-based publishing company, *Writing for the Lord* Ministries); as a former radio and television host; and in several leadership positions within the local church, the Christian publishing industry, and the National Association of the Church of God (Anderson, Indiana).

A native of Richmond, Virginia, Johnson was introduced to the Bible and the Christian doctrine as a child and active member of Ebenezer Baptist Church. At the age of eight, his maternal grandmother (Granny), a devout Seventh Day Adventist, prophesied that he would preach the gospel in due season. From these planted seeds, Johnson, alongside his wife, Gail, confessed Jesus Christ as their personal Lord and Savior on May 2, 1993. This spiritual transformation occurred slightly less than two months after their marriage on March 6, 1993.

An active member of the Purpose Management Team and Pastor of Discipleship at Celebration Church, Columbia, Maryland, Pastor Johnson oversees the following ministries: Intercessory prayer, prison (men and women), Christian education (Bible Institute), Christian guidance, writers, and the Good 4 U Health and Wellness. He also serves as Secretary, National Association of the Church of God Men's Ministry (2009 to present). Johnson was initially ordained into the Christian ministry as a deacon in 2000 while at Shiloh Pentecostal Church, Incorporated, *Christian Love Center*, Somerville, New Jersey, with his wife. He is an Evangelical Training Association (ETA) certified instructor (2000 to present).

Johnson is a professional in government as well as private industry. For twenty-seven years, he has performed successfully in numerous middle and senior-level positions in the areas of workforce development, training, organizational change, acquisition/procurement, customer service, client relationships, and program management, to include the Department of Defense, Department of the Treasury, the Government of the District of Columbia, Administrative Office of the U.S. Courts, Department of the Army, Defense Logistics Agency, and in the private sector at Vivendi Universal and Reuters America. He has testified before the United States House of Representatives Committee on Small Business, and has prepared testimony that was presented before the District of Columbia Committee on Government Operations. Johnson is a graduate of the U.S. Department of Agriculture Graduate School's Executive Potential Program (1996). During this program, he assisted the Office of Federal Procurement Policy with several procurement reform initiatives that were tied to the National Performance Review under the Clinton Administration. In 1999, he was awarded the distinction of *"Fellow"* by the National Contract Management Association Board of Directors.

Pastor Johnson is the eldest son of Ernest and the late Adele Johnson. He attended and graduated from the Richmond Public School system and Virginia Commonwealth University earning a B.S. degree in Business Administration and Management/Economics/Finance. He also completed course work towards a MBA degree at Marymount University and the University of Colorado at Colorado Springs. In 2002, Johnson graduated from the True Disciple Ministries Bible Institute, Somerville, New Jersey, earning three Church Ministries Certifications through ETA, Wheaton, Illinois. Johnson lives in Clarksville, Maryland, with his wife and three teen-aged sons, Kevin, Christopher, and Cameron.

<u>To order additional copies of this book:</u>

Give God the Glory!

Called to be *Light* in the Workplace—A Workbook

© 2013, Book #8
ISBN: 978-0-9705902-7-5
Price: $15.00
Pages: 236
Dimensions: 8.5" x 11"
Paperback

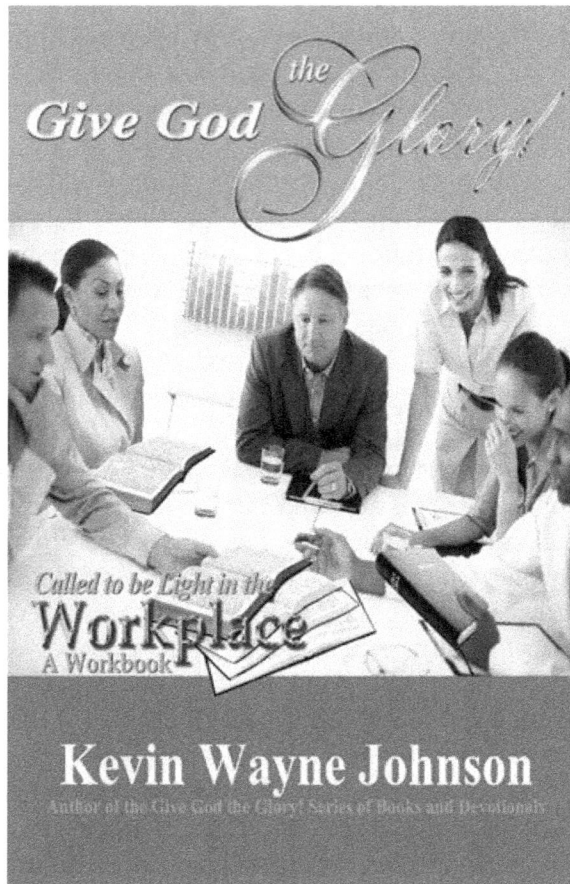

Name: _____

Address: _____

City: _____

State/Zip Code: _____

E-mail: _____

Mail order form with check or money order to: *Writing for the Lord* Ministries, 6400 Shannon Court, Clarksville, MD 21029. Please add $3.00 for shipping and handling. We also accept payment through PayPal: KGJ27@aol.com.

These series of books are available everywhere that books are sold OR order here:

Winner of eighteen literary/media awards, 2001—present

Give God the Glory!

Let Your Light So Shine, a devotional/gift book

© 2012 (Revised/Reprinted), Book #3

Third Printing

ISBN: 978-0-9883038-0-5

Price: $5.00

Pages: 54

Dimensions: 5.06" x 7.81"

Paperback

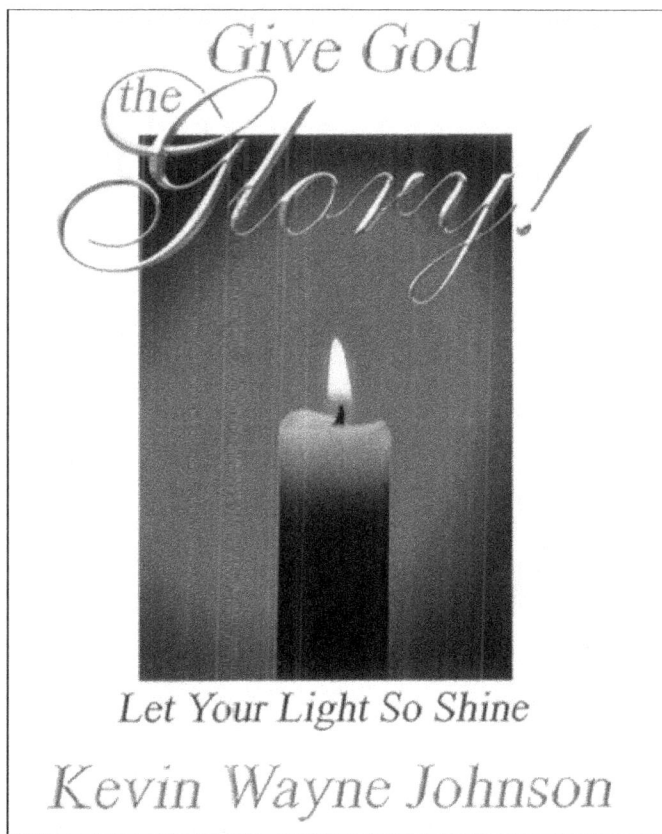

Name: _____

Address: _____

City: _____

State/Zip Code: _____

E-mail: _____

Mail order form with check or money order to: *Writing for the Lord* Ministries, 6400 Shannon Court, Clarksville, MD 21029. Please add $3.00 for shipping and handling. We also accept payment through PayPal: KGJ27@aol.com.

Give God the Glory!
Know God & Do the Will of God Concerning Your Life
(Revised Edition)

© 2011, Book #1
ISBN: 978-0-9705902-6-8
Price: $10.99
Pages: 193
Dimensions: 5.5" x 8.5"
Paperback

Name: _____

Address: _____

City: _____

State/Zip Code: _____

E-mail: _____

Mail order form with check or money order to: *Writing for the Lord* Ministries, 6400 Shannon Court, Clarksville, MD 21029. Please add $3.00 for shipping and handling. We also accept payment through PayPal: KGJ27@aol.com.

Give God the Glory!
The Power in the Local Church
© 2010, Book #7
ISBN: 978-0-9705902-5-1
Price: $19.95
Pages: 183
Dimensions: 6" x 9"
Hardback

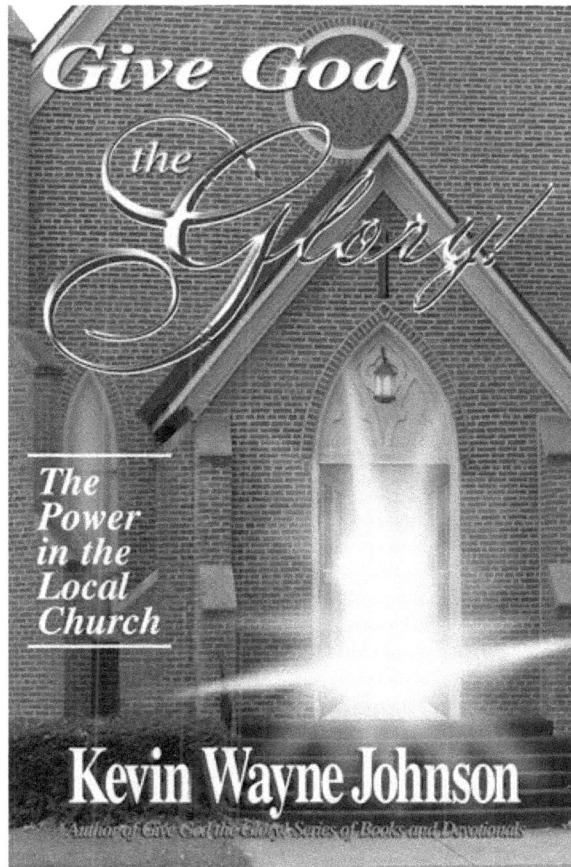

Name: _____

Address: _____

City: _____

State/Zip Code: _____

E-mail: _____

Mail order form with check or money order to: *Writing for the Lord* Ministries, 6400 Shannon Court, Clarksville, MD 21029. Please add $3.00 for shipping and handling. We also accept payment through PayPal: KGJ27@aol.com.

Give God the Glory! STUDY GUIDE
Know God & Do the Will of God Concerning <u>Your</u> Life

© 2008, Book #6
ISBN: 978-0-9705902-2-0
Price: $15.00
Pages: 133
Dimensions: 8.5" x 11"
Paperback

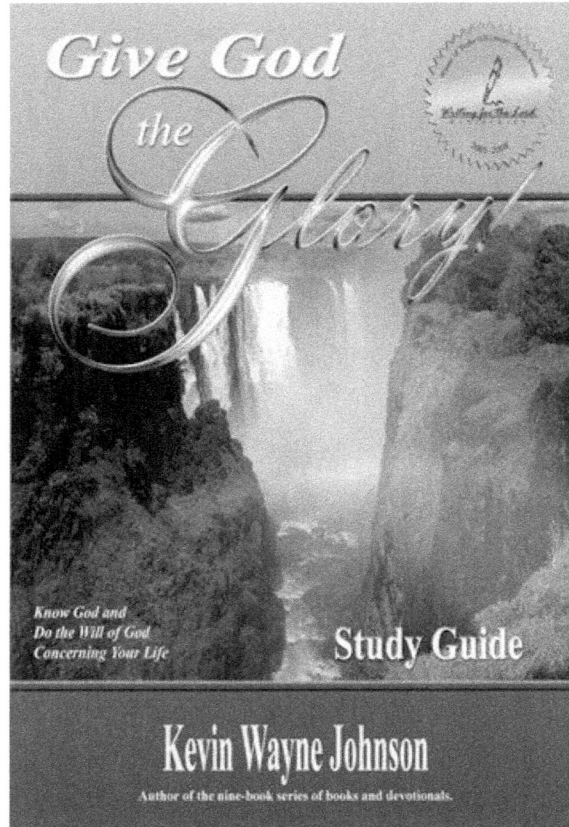

Name: _____

Address: _____

City: _____

State/Zip Code: _____

E-mail: _____

Mail order form with check or money order to: *Writing for the Lord* Ministries, 6400 Shannon Court, Clarksville, MD 21029. Please add $3.00 for shipping and handling. We also accept payment through PayPal: KGJ27@aol.com.

Give God the Glory!
Your Role in Your Family, a devotional/gift book

© 2006, Book #5
First Printing
ISBN: 978-0-9705902-4-4
Price: $5.00
Pages: 56
Dimensions: 5.06" x 7.81"
Paperback

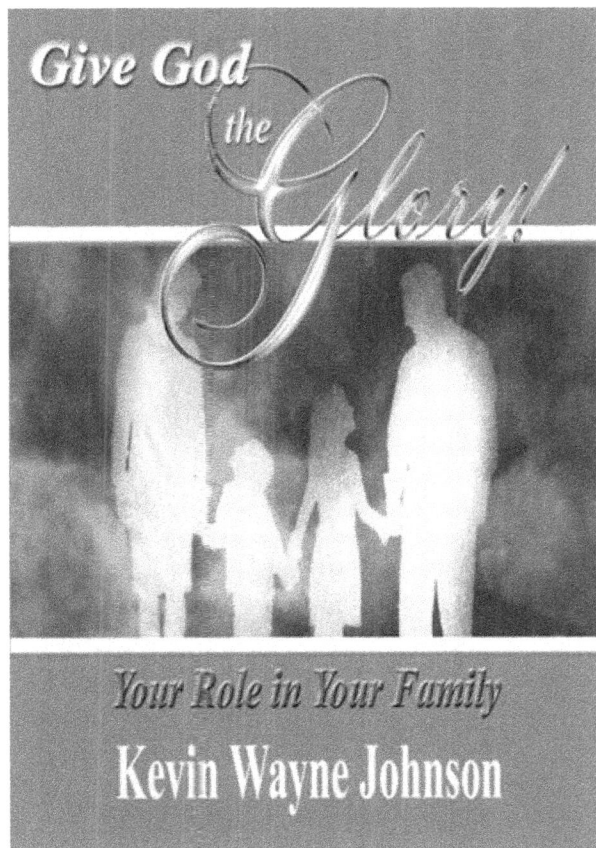

Name: _____

Address: _____

City: _____

State/Zip Code: _____

E-mail: _____

Mail order form with check or money order to: *Writing for the Lord* Ministries, 6400 Shannon Court, Clarksville, MD 21029. Please add $3.00 for shipping and handling. We also accept payment through PayPal: KGJ27@aol.com.

Give God the Glory!
The Godly Family Life

© 2005, Book #4
Second Printing
ISBN: 978-0-9705902-3-7
Price: $13.00
Pages: 200
Dimensions: 6" x 9"
Paperback

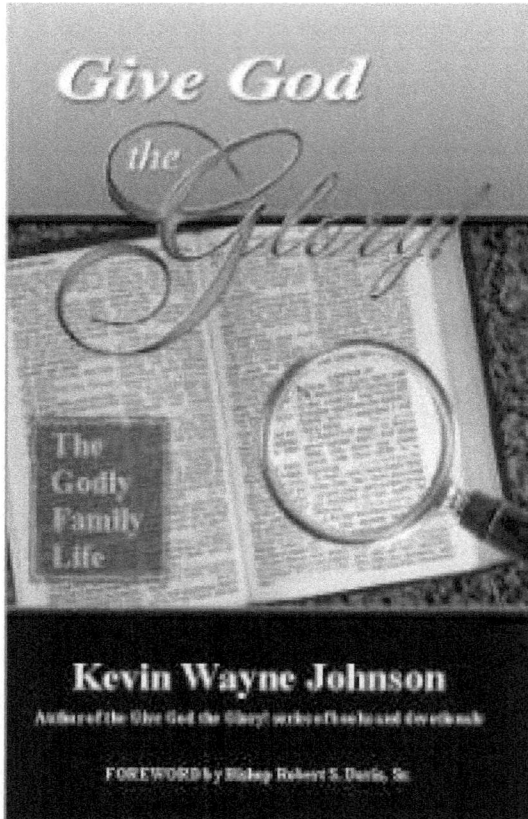

Name: _____

Address: _____

City: _____

State/Zip Code: _____

E-mail: _____

Mail order form with check or money order to: *Writing for the Lord* Ministries, 6400 Shannon Court, Clarksville, MD 21029. Please add $3.00 for shipping and handling. We also accept payment through PayPal: KGJ27@aol.com.

Give God the Glory!
Called to be *Light* in the Workplace

© 2003, Book #2
Second Printing
ISBN: 978-0-9705902-1-3
Price: $14.95
Pages: 185
Dimensions: 6" x 9"
Paperback

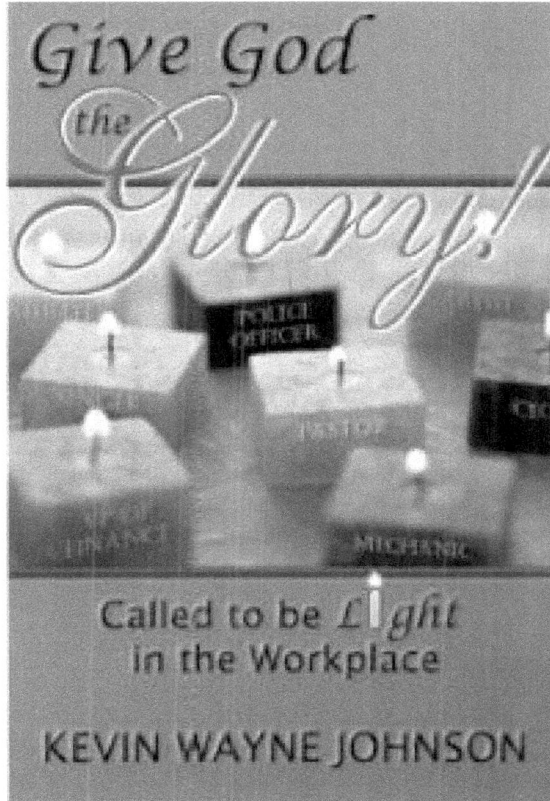

Name: _____

Address: _____

City: _____

State/Zip Code: _____

E-mail: _____

Mail order form with check or money order to: *Writing for the Lord* Ministries, 6400 Shannon Court, Clarksville, MD 21029. Please add $3.00 for shipping and handling. We also accept payment through PayPal: KGJ27@aol.com.

Other books featuring Kevin Wayne Johnson's writings:

Blended Families: An Anthology
© 2006
2008 Christian Small Publishers Association
Non-Fiction Book of the Year

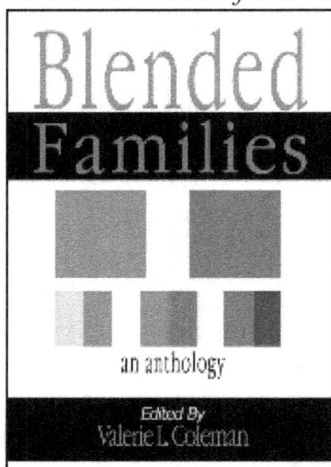

ISBN: 978-0-9786066-0-2
Price $14.95
Paperback

The Secret: His Word Impacting Our Lives
© 2007

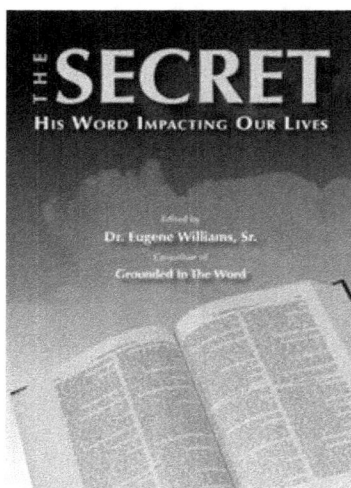

ISBN: 978-0-6151797-6-6
Price: $12.95
Paperback

To order, visit our online bookstore at:
www.writingforthelord.com /
www.writingforthelord.org

No Limits ... No Boundaries
Marketing Your Book around the Globe
(with Antonio Crawford for the Annual National
Christian Writer's Conference)
© 2009

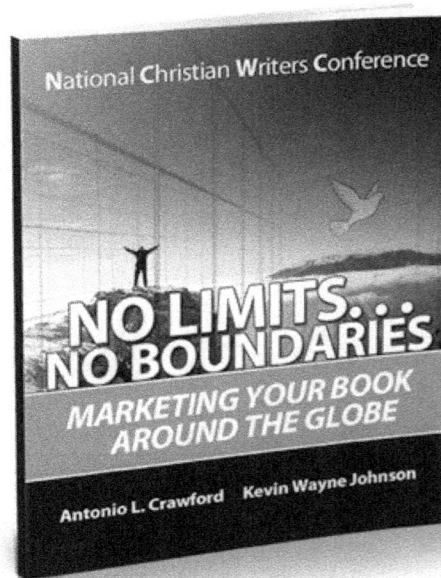

e-book
To order, visit our online bookstore at:
www.writingforthelord.com /
www.writingforthelord.org

"This then is the message which we have heard of him, and declare unto you, that God is **light***, and in him is no darkness at all.*

—1 John 1:5 KJV

Amen.

* 9 7 8 0 9 7 0 5 9 0 2 7 5 *